WINGS OVER IDAHO

For Robert R. Auth

Right: DeLloyd Thompson flew into the home stretch ahead of Barney Oldfield, Boise fairgrounds, 1915.

ISHS 62-19.1121

WINGS OVER IDAHO

AN AVIATION HISTORY

Arthur A. Hart

Caxton Press
Caldwell, Idaho, 2008

Copyright 1991 by Arthur Hart

All rights reserved. No part of this book may be reproduced in any manner without the express written consent of the publisher, except in the case of brief excerpts in critical reviews and articles. All inquiries should be addressed to Caxton Press, 312 Main Street, Caldwell, ID 83605.

Originally published by Historic Boise, Inc. in 1991, made possible in part by a grant from the Boise Airport Commission.

ISBN 0-978-0-87004-467-0

Library of Congress Cataloging-in-Publication Data

Hart, Arthur A.
Wings over Idaho : an aviation history / Arthur A. Hart.
p. cm.
Originally published: Boise, Idaho : Historic Boise, Inc., c1991.
Includes bibliographical references and index.
ISBN 978-0-87004-467-0 (pbk.)
1. Aeronautics--Idaho--History. I. Title.

TL522.I3H37 2008
629.1309796--dc22

2008019827

Right: Walter Brookins, in a Wright Brothers pusher, flew at the Boise fairgrounds on April 20, 1911.

Printed and bound in the United States of America
CAXTON PRESS
Caldwell, Idaho 176669

CONTENTS

ISHS 70-114.4

FOREWORD

This book began as a modest overview of the history of aviation in Boise, Idaho. It grew, inevitably it seemed, into a history of aviation embracing the whole state. This was due, in part, to the revolution created by flight itself – the wonder that made Idaho's thousands of square miles of mountains and wilderness passable by plane in hours rather than weeks. Not only could pioneer pilots fly into towns all over the state, but national and international aviation figures came to Idaho as well.

This is still an overview of a story worthy of many books, but it is a beginning. Hopefully, others will take up the needed and fascinating task of researching in depth the history of aviation in every Idaho town and region. There are great stories still to be told.

Arthur A. Hart

UP, UP, AND AWAY

I

The earliest man-made wings over Idaho were kites, probably those flown by Chinese residents in whose culture kite making and kite flying were ancient pastimes. Kites in the form of birds, fish and dragons had been flown in the Orient for thousands of years — long before Europeans took an interest. It was not until the 18th Century that kites were much used in Europe and America, and then for scientific purposes — an innovation sparked by Benjamin Franklin with his celebrated experiments with lightning.

Boise boys and girls flew kites in the 19th Century, although newspaper references to them are rare. We do have one brief item from 1882, telling us that "the kite flying time seems to be passing without much attention."[1] The kites flown by Idaho children would almost certainly have followed the diamond shape most common in 19th Century America, balanced by a tail of knotted rags. Another 1882 item noted that "A China kite representing a hawk, away up in the air, attracted considerable attention yesterday afternoon."[2]

Kites for meteorological observation were developed in the latter part of the 19th Century, after experiments for military purposes in the American Civil War. These were box kites — open frames like boxes, covered with fabric except at the ends through which air could pass to give them lift. Very large box kites were used in Idaho in the early 20th Century for making aerial photographs. C.L. Huntington took aerial views of Boise in December, 1909, by sending his camera aloft in a box kite ten feet long and five and a half feet high.[3] Cameras were tripped by a line to the ground or by a timing mechanism. H.V. Lee, another barnstorming box kite photographer, also took aerial panoramas of Boise in 1909.[4]

ISHS 80-32.18

Aeronaut William Goda flew his hot air balloon at Nez Perce in about 1914.

The earliest manned flights in Idaho were by "aeronauts," the name applied in early days to those who flew in balloons. (Only later would it be applied to pilots of planes). In the year Boise's new Natatorium opened its doors, 1892, a team of aeronauts entertained crowds with balloon ascensions and parachute jumps at the big pleasure palace east of the city. On August 29, 1892, Professor Thomas Godfrey took his hot air balloon up a thousand feet and parachuted out as it drifted toward Table Rock and the Idaho Penitentiary.[5] Godfrey also demonstrated his skill and nerve as a high-wire walker at the "Nat" and in front of the Overland Hotel at the corner of 8th and Main.[6]

Although hot air balloons had been flown since 1783, when the Montgolfier brothers of France launched their first one,[7] and in America since 1793, a flight watched by President George Washington at Philadelphia,[8] they were a great novelty in Idaho in the 1890s. Since observation balloons had been used by both North and South in the Civil War,[9] it is likely that some of Boise's veterans of that war had seen

ISHS 61-65.1

ISHS 61-65.2

William Lester and E.J. Parker flew this hydrogen blimp at Boise's polo grounds on October 19, 1908.

them before, but for most people, this was their first sight of men aloft.

In 1908 the celebrated Strobel airship came to Boise to perform at the Idaho State Fair. As a preview of its local appearance, the *Idaho Statesman* ran a picture of it as it had looked at the Minnesota State Fair earlier in the year.[10] It showed a strange sausage-shaped gas bag with a rickety open-framed structure dangling beneath it. The pilot sat in a saddle astride this skeletal "horse." Power was supplied by a four cylinder gasoline engine which turned a nine-foot sheet metal propeller, and steering was accomplished by manipulating a six-foot square rudder of the same material. Earlier balloons to appear in Boise had used hot air to achieve buoyancy. The Strobel airship used hydrogen gas — the dangerous, flammable substance remembered today as the cause of the fiery destruction in 1937 of the great German dirigible *Hindenburg* at Lakehurst, New Jersey.[11] Helium gas, available only in America, was used in most American airships for safety, even though it was much more expensive and somewhat less efficient than hydrogen.[12]

Where could barnstorming aeronauts like William T. Lester and E.J. Parker get hydrogen gas in an isolated place like Boise, Idaho? Why, make it themselves, of course! The *Statesman* described the process:

"Yesterday, Mr. Lester made arrangements to secure from the Baxter iron foundry 2500 pounds of steel and iron borings, which will be used to generate gas with which to inflate the big bag . . . hydrogen gas, generated from scrap iron dissolved in sulphuric acid, is used in the big gas bag. Mr. Lester personally supervises the making of the gas, for the manufacture of which he has an up-to-date scientific outfit. The silk receptacle has a capacity of 8000 cubic feet". . .[13]

Delayed a day by strong winds that made it too dangerous to fly, Captain Parker made two flights at the fairgrounds track on October 19, 1908: "The maneuvers of the apparatus awed the crowd which lined the fences around the circuit, and Captain Parker was frequently cheered when he made the ship execute 'figure eights' and other difficult evolutions."[14]

Crude though it was, the Strobel airship was the forerunner of the popular Goodyear blimps so widely used today for aerial coverage of televised athletic events world-wide. They all use non-flammable helium, their crews don't have to make it themselves, and get to ride in comfortable enclosed gondolas. But, like Captain Parker, pilots of modern blimps head for cover when winds and lightning make flying too dangerous.

Hot air balloons continued to come to Idaho towns in the years that followed the Strobel airship's 1908 flights. They were similar to the balloons flown at the Boise Natatorium in

ISHS

Boise's great Natatorium was the site of numerous balloon ascensions in the late 1890s and early 1900s.

1892, and parachute jumps were usually included as part of the show. It was dangerous work. On June 24, 1911, aeronaut R.J. O'Donnell, while performing for the Miller Carnival Company at Weiser, landed in the Snake River and drowned.[15] Another balloonist, who billed himself as "Daredevil Kohl," performed "thrilling and sensational acts," at White City Park near the Boise Natatorium in 1915 and 1918. On September 1, 1918, Kohl landed in the Boise River when he misjudged his leap with a parachute. "Not being able to swim a stroke, Cole (sic) had a mental cold bath as well as a literal one. His first instinct was to put his feet down, and to his surprise they struck bottom and he was able to wade in to shore. Cole, it is said, has already engaged for swimming lessons at the Natatorium this week."[16]

Veteran balloonist R.C. Thurman from Anderson, Indiana, worked the western states in 1922. A mailing piece sent to the managers of fairs that year said, "Going Up Is My Business," and proclaimed Thurman to be owner of "The best equipped balloon outfit used by balloonists on the road. I use the latest patent hold downs and patent inflators. I can fill my balloon on paved streets, parks, lawns or court house lawns, with no damage thereto, as I dig no trench like others do. I give nice high rides and do no 'stalling'."[17] Thurman spent more than a month at White City Park in July and August, 1922, making regular evening ascents followed by parachute drops from about 2,000 feet. On one occasion he was painfully injured, but came back for the next performance like the trouper he was. Since Thurman's was a one-man show, after he made his leap into space, the hot air balloon sometimes drifted nearly 10 miles before "it finally upended and dropped into a field."[18]

Two men with Idaho connections made international ballooning history in the 1920s and '30s. Captain Hawthorne C. Gray, who had been a commissioned officer in the Idaho National Guard, set a new world altitude record of 42,470 feet on May 4, 1927. In 1926 he had won second place in the famous Gordon Bennett balloon races. He has been called by ballooning historians the most illustrious aeronaut of his day.[19]

Albert W. Stevens, who had worked for eight years as electrical superintendent for the Boston and Idaho Gold Dredging Company at Grimes Pass in Boise Basin,[20] was part of the three-man team that flew the hydrogen balloon *Explorer I* to the new world record height of 60,613 feet on July 28, 1934.[21] On November 11, 1935, he and O.A. Anderson surpassed that record with an ascension of 72,395 feet in *Explorer II*.[22] These two National Geographic Society-sponsored flights made Captain Stevens America's most famous balloonist.

Idaho had seen Stevens often in the 1920s before he turned to ballooning. He set a new world record for parachutists with a jump of four-and-a-half miles above McCook Field near Dayton, Ohio, in June, 1922.[23] In September, 1923, he landed in Boise with Lt. John A. Macready. The two were on an aerial photographic mission to Yellowstone Park and the Teton Range and were next headed for San Diego to attempt to photograph a September 10th eclipse of the sun.[24]

In 1925 Macready and Stevens made national headlines when they were reported lost in the Amazon Jungle while on another photography mission, but turned up safe a few days later.[25] In September, 1925, the two were again in Boise, this time to photograph Idaho mountain scenery. Stevens was chief of the Army Air Corps photo section at McCook Field, on assignment to record America's national parks and scenic wonders from the air for an exhibit to open at Philadelphia on July 4, 1926 — the 150th anniversary of the signing of the Declaration of Independence.[26]

Macready, flying a DeHavilland 4 biplane on this occasion, was already famous in his own right for his non-stop flight from New York to San Diego May 2-3, 1923, with Lt. Oakley G. Kelly in a Fokker T-2. This was the first non-stop flight across the country.[27]

A new age of hot air ballooning for sport would come to Idaho half a century after Thurman — one in which many local amateurs participated. That will be described later.

ISHS 73-205.3

The ill-fated Bleriot Monoplane that almost made Idaho's first airplane flight was under repair when this photo was made in October, 1910.

DARING YOUNG MEN, AND A GIRL II

On December 17, 1903, Orville Wright flew the world's first powered, heavier-than-air craft in the sand dunes at Kitty Hawk, North Carolina. He and brother Wilbur had worked for years to develop the first successful airplane, beginning with box kites and working their way step by step through a series of gliders to that first powered flight. It was decided by the toss of a coin that Orville would fly first, but history properly records the milestone as an equal achievement of the two brothers.[1]

By 1910 the Wrights had trained a group of pilots who could demonstrate and promote the planes they were building and continually improving. Wright fliers took their fragile craft across the country by railroad in unassembled form, put them together, and flew at county fairs or anywhere else that might draw sufficient crowds to publicize the new air age.[2] Glenn Curtiss, the Wrights' chief competitor in this pioneer phase of exploiting the airplane, also trained pilots and sent them out for traveling exhibitions.[3] Both companies would send planes to Idaho for the first successful flights seen in the Gem State.

In 1910, N.A. Brown, a Tacoma businessman, almost beat Curtiss and the Wright Brothers to the punch. He shipped a Bleriot monoplane to Boise to be flown at the Idaho Intermountain Fair.[4] The pilot was A.C. Tunnison, a mechanical engineer who had made improvements and modifications on the famous Bleriot XI design with which Louis Bleriot had made history by flying across the English Channel from Calais to Dover on July 5, 1909.[5] The Tacoma plane was larger than the Bleriot XI and, with a 90 horsepower engine, considerably more powerful. Tunnison had cracked up with minor damage at Walla Walla using a 60 horsepower engine in an earlier test. The repaired plane with the new 90 horses was expected to do much better.[6]

Alas — it was not to be. Despite the enthusiasm and optimism of owner, pilot and fair directors, everything went wrong. The *Statesman* headline said it all — "AEROPLANE IS HUGE SUCCESS EXCEPT THAT IT UTTERLY REFUSES TO FLY." On Tunnison's first attempted takeoff the Bleriot's wheels ran into a small irrigation ditch and the little monoplane never got off the ground.[7] On October 15, 1910, nearly three weeks after the plane's coming was announced, and while Boiseans eagerly awaited history in the making, the *Statesman* reported "AEROPLANE FLIGHTS THING OF PAST." A writ of attachment was granted on the engine and propeller to the supplier who had not been paid. Plane owner Brown, said the paper, "completely lost heart and decamped in great disgust with himself and the machine which refused to fly." The *Statesman* expressed the feelings of disappointed thousands of fairgoers when it proclaimed the whole experience "a fiasco."[8]

At the same time, preparations were being made in Lewiston for the arrival of James Ward and a Curtiss biplane scheduled to fly at the Lewiston-Clarkston Fair. By coincidence, both Lewiston and Boise flights were scheduled for October 10-15, 1910. The Boise promoters had even been optimistic enough to run an ad in the *Lewiston Morning Tribune* proclaiming the ill-fated Bleriot "the first air ship ever in Idaho."[9]

This time, the sectional laurels clearly went to Lewiston, for despite the difficult logistics involved in such early exhibitions, James Ward did indeed make the first airplane flight in

ISHS 78-203.96

J.J. Ward made the first successful airplane flight in Idaho at Lewiston on October 13, 1910. This photo was made next day, and on the following day Ward crashed, demolishing the plane.

Idaho.[10] Specifications for the runway from which the Curtiss ship would take off and land were received, and a smooth strip was built immediately in front of the main grandstand. On October 5 the Fair Association received a telegram from the Curtiss company in Chicago: "James Ward, the aviator, and his Curtiss flying machine leave here early today for Lewiston. Have very short time to put machine together after its arrival, so please cooperate with us. Advertise flying machine big. It always draws big crowds."[11] The message also asked that a tent be erected and ready to house the plane and the crew that would assemble and maintain it during fair week.

For the Lewiston-Clarkston Fair Association this was indeed "the greatest undertaking" in its history, "the attraction being secured at very heavy expense." The *Tribune* considered the Lewiston area an ideal location for the flights: "Sheltered by the high hills, the Lewiston-Clarkston valley offers an exceptionally good aviation field for successful and spectacular flights."[12]

Promotion of the Lewiston flights was all that the Curtiss company could have wished. Several photographs of pilot Ward and his plane appeared in the *Morning Tribune* in the days before his arrival.[13] Curiously, one of the ads showed what was evidently a stock cut of a Bleriot monoplane instead of the Curtiss biplane, with the message, "Take a look at Darius Green and his flying machine at the Fair Grounds every day next week."[14] The reference to "Darius Green" was one most readers of the day would have understood, since the humorous poem about a "country dunce" who tried to fly with disastrous results was part of popular culture in the years before anyone had flown.[15]

Aviator James J. Ward, who would make the first airplane flight in Idaho, was interviewed several times while the plane was being made ready. Readers learned that he was the "official aeronautical instructor" of the Illinois Aeronautical Club of Chicago, and had once made a flight of 25 miles and reached an altitude of 2,200 feet. He had made over 100 flights and never had an accident. He assured reporters he had no anxiety about flying provided he was at least 200 feet above the ground when something went wrong, since he was sure he could land safely from that height. "Most of the serious accidents have happened when the trouble occurred when the machine was about 50 feet from the ground," he said.[16]

After a series of tests of the engine and short runs along the taxi strip, Ward made the first takeoff ever witnessed in Idaho on Thursday, October 13, 1910. Engine trouble caused a rough landing that demolished the front wheel on one occasion, but since it was a standard bicycle wheel, a replacement was soon found. On October 14, pilot Ward proclaimed the weather ideal for flying, and made several flights that thrilled the crowd. "The cheers that floated to his ears from the grandstand as he twice passed by in his bird machine must have convinced him that he had made good," said the *Tribune.*[17]

On October 15, 1910, a special dispatch went out from Lewiston: "The Curtiss biplane with which J.J. Ward of Chicago has been making daily flights at the fair, tonight lies a heap of junk on the banks of the Snake River, and that Ward himself is not in the morgue or at the hospital, is almost a miracle." After his engine stopped dead some 200 feet above the ground, Ward might still have brought the plane in safely had not the forward control collapsed totally. Ward escaped with only a sprained ankle and bruised wrist by jumping clear of the plane just before it hit.[18]

ISHS 700

Lewiston saw aviation history in the making -- first in 1904 with Captain Winslow, and then in 1910 with J.J. Ward.

ISHS 78-203.4

Captain Stewart V. Winslow risked his neck trying to get this home-made bicycle-powered glider off the ground at Lewiston, July 30, 1904.

Lewiston had seen one earlier attempt at manned flight. On July 30, 1904, Captain Stewart V. Winslow, a riverboat pilot, pedaled his bicycle-powered "airship" downhill toward a cliff on the Lewiston side of the Snake River, hoping to sail across to Clarkston, Washington. It was fortunate for Winslow that the front bike wheel collapsed before he got airborne, for he would probably have been killed.[19] Although a planned second attempt never came off, the Winslow machine was remembered years later when French aviation pioneer Robert Esnault-Pelterie sued the United States government for patent infringement, claiming that it was he who had invented the single-stick airplane control, widely used and known as a "joy stick" by U.S. fliers. High ranking officers of the armed forces visited Lewiston to investigate Winslow's 1904 flight, hoping to prove that he had used a single-stick control before the Frenchman did. There was not enough left of the old ship to prove anything one way or the other, and the United States eventually paid Esnault-Pelterie several million dollars.[20]

Captain Winslow, in his eighties, was an honored guest at the dedication of Lewiston's new County-City airport on June 1, 1952.[21]

Boise's first look at flying came the following spring. Walter Brookins, head of the Wright Brothers' flying school, took off on the dark and windy afternoon of April 19, 1911, before only a few spectators at the Intermountain fairgrounds. The newspaper reporter was impressed: "Brookins flew. He demonstrated to the absolute satisfaction of some 200 people who watched him at the fairgrounds about 5 o'clock in the afternoon that flying is not a dream, but a reality."[22] Next day, both Curtiss and Wright fliers took to the air before 3,000 people at the Intermountain Fair.[23] Walter Brookins, who had received much fanfare as the Wright Brothers' representative, appeared as scheduled, but Eugene Ely, noted Curtiss flier who had achieved fame by landing a plane on the deck of the battleship *Pennsylvania* on January 18, 1911,[24] was replaced on the Boise program at the last minute by Charles Willard, "Dean of Aviators." Willard was the first pilot trained by Glenn Curtiss, and claimed to be the first man ever to make a flight of over a mile.[25] In those palmy days a pilot could be proclaimed "dean" of fliers with less than two years experience. Some of the best didn't last that long.

Barnstorming in Curtiss and Wright planes at that time was mortally dangerous. Already two of the greatest of the early fliers had plunged to their deaths before the horrified eyes of large crowds. Ralph Johnstone crashed at Denver on November 20, 1910, and Archie Hoxsey at Los Angeles on December 31 that year.[26] It was Hoxsey who had taken ex-

ISHS 78-94.11

Walter Brookins flew his Wright Brothers modified Model B at Boise's Intermountain fairgrounds on April 20, 1911.

President Theodore Roosevelt aloft at St. Louis in October, 1910. Roosevelt was the first American chief executive to fly. "Teddy" thought the experience so "bully" that he courted disaster by waving to the crowds with both hands. The pilot was worried that he might fall out of the plane or get a hand in the engine rotating at his side. "Keep your hands on the rail, Colonel," he ordered, and Roosevelt, after one last wave, obeyed.[27]

Lincoln Beachey, son of Idaho stagecoach king and folk hero Hill Beachey, usually considered the most daring and reckless of them all, plunged to his death in San Francisco Bay in 1915 before 50,000 spectators.[28]

A favorite stunt of early barnstorming fliers was to race against motorcycles or automobiles. In 1911 at the Boise fair Walter Brookins took on Frank Irving "at the wheel of one of the speediest Buick racing cars ever seen in the northwest."[29] This was billed as a grudge match between the two for a side bet of $1,000, but that was probably part of the promotion. High poles with colored flags on top were placed at the four corners of the dirt track, and Brookins had to make his turns outside them.[30] The two raced to a tie on April 21, 1911. Irving had been clocked at over 60 miles per hour in 1910, and the planes of the day could go only slightly faster. The wide turns the plane was forced to make made it about even, but like good showmen, all competitors in these exhibitions realized that the public would lose interest as soon as the planes began to win regularly.

Alys McKey became the first woman to fly in Idaho on May 30, 1913, when she took off in a Curtiss biplane at the Boise fairgrounds. Twenty minutes earlier she had experienced a minor accident that saved her life. In the press of the crowd that gathered round the frail plane, someone had leaned hard enough on a wing rod to crack it. It might never have been noticed but on her first attempted takeoff she hit a rut in the field. "That jolt saved my life," she said. It collapsed the top wing onto the one beneath. "If I had started on the smooth track, instead of inside the field the jar would not have happened and I would have left the ground with that rod already splintered . . . with it in that condition the first time I attempted a turn in the air would have snapped it and that would have been the death of me."[31]

Alys was barnstorming with young Milton "Johnny" Bryant. She looked "more like a high

ISHS 61-121.34

ISHS 62-19.1104

ISHS 62-19.1106

Top: The crowd at Boise fairgrounds is watching Walter Brookins in his Wright plane, as Charles Willard and his Curtiss wait their turn in the infield.

Middle: Charles Willard, "Dean of Aviators," with his Curtiss pusher, Boise, April, 1911.

Bottom: An eager crowd of men and boys rushes to greet Walter Brookins as he dismounts from his Wright machine.

ISHS 62-19.1111

ISHS 62-19.1105

Top: Walter Brookins and a passenger at Boise, April, 1911. Few people would risk it. Above: The Wright Brothers modified Model B that flew at Boise, April, 1911.

ISHS 62-19.1120

Barney Oldfield rounds the turn at the fairgrounds track going more than 60 miles an hour, but DeLloyd Thompson is about to pass him, June, 1915. Note the mid-wing ailerons.

school girl about to graduate than a seasoned aviatrix," wrote a reporter.[32] The two fliers were married while in Boise,[33] and told the press they hoped to be back in the fall if they secured a contract to fly at the Intermountain Fair.[34] It was not to be, for Johnny Bryant was killed two months later at Victoria, British Columbia.[35] Alys McKey had told Boise reporters in May "I never make a flight, of course, without figuring before I start that it may be my last. Life insurance companies refuse to insure us but that is part of the profession we follow."[36] The courageous young woman, so soon to be widowed, expressed eloquently the fatalism that went with early day flying.

In 1915 Boise was treated to a series of races at the fair featuring the acknowledged leader of daredevil drivers, Barney Oldfield, and a recent sensation in flying, DeLloyd Thompson, billed in "show-biz" hyperbole as "World's Greatest Aviator."[37] Claiming that many concerned people had begged the flier not to perform the dreaded "tumble flight" that had killed Lincoln Beachey, Thompson's manager said he would absolutely perform it in Boise anyhow. Another name for the stunt was the "Undertaker's Drop."[38]

When Barney Oldfield came to Boise in

ISHS 62-19.1115

DeLloyd Thompson landing in front of the fairgrounds grandstand, June 24, 1915. Had he missed "there would have been many a first class funeral in Idaho."

1915 he had just set a new record of 111.5 miles per hour at Chicago. Thompson, at the same show, had looped-the-loop 53 times in succession.[39] Their race was promoted as "for the championship of the universe." The familiar face of Oldfield chewing the stub of a cigar that was his trademark, appeared in a life-size cut on page one of the *Statesman* sports section. He told reporters that for 15 years he had always driven with a cigar in his teeth because it kept his mouth moist. Without it, wrote one newsman, the great Oldfield looked like a bank president.[40]

Boise Mayor Robinson proclaimed a half-holiday for Thursday, June 24, 1915.[41] "Oldfield Day" drew the largest crowd ever gathered in the city, according to the newspapers: 3,500 were carried to the fairground by the streetcars, 700 came in automobiles, and it was estimated that 2,000 came from out of town. The crowd was so dense that the *Statesman* observed "If aviator Thompson had accidentally sideswiped the row of boxes in front of the grandstand there would have been many a first class funeral in Idaho."[42]

With aircraft taking a dramatic part in World War I then raging in Europe, part of DeLloyd Thompson's act, "from his position in the skies," was to drop "pseudo bombs" on a "fort" that had been set up on the track. To give a realistic effect, men on the ground launched fireworks that exploded in air as the plane whizzed by. "The fort was soon on fire and the aviator 'descended within the lines,' as they say in Europe," wrote the *Statesman*. "Then came the rush and the dust as hundreds of cars poked their way out of the grounds. Everybody was happy and dusty. They had seen a great exhibition, such as their forebears never dreamed of a few years ago."[43]

ISHS 62-19.1121

Barney Oldfield, world's greatest racing driver, and DeLloyd Thompson, "world's greatest aviator," compete for "the championship of the universe," Boise, 1915.

ISHS 62-19.1116

Oldfield's racing car carried an ad for Firestone tires, "My only life insurance." His mechanic looks drenched in oil.

By 1915 many Idaho towns had been treated to the thrill of aerial exhibitions. The Glenn Curtiss company had sent representatives, and a number of private aviation companies using his planes were in the business of working the county fair circuit.

Silas Christofferson, in a Curtiss pusher, flew at Ontario, Oregon, Caldwell, and Emmett in the fall of 1912. Advance publicity credited him with "the world's record for a sustained flight for distance" from Portland to Vancouver, British Columbia, and he had recently taken off from the roof of a Portland hotel. All went well at Ontario and Caldwell, but in landing at Emmett he ran into a fence and wrecked the plane.[44]

Dr. Frank J. Bell, another Curtiss flyer, appeared at Twin Falls September 19 and 20, 1913. His afternoon flights from the ballpark followed a baseball game to which fans paid 50 cents admission. Of course, anybody in the area could see the plane fly free, but the promoters pointed out the advantage of a seat in the stands: "The starting and lighting of an aeroplane is fully as great a sight as to see one in actual flight in the air. One does not get a correct idea of what they are and how they work without seeing the start and finish."[45] Pilot Bell's schedule called for an appearance at Oakley and a flight from Burley to Albion.[46]

ISHS 73-221.180

Dr. Frank Bell flew this Curtiss pusher at Twin Falls, September 19-20, 1913.

ISHS 79-141.38/c

Frank Bryant gave Coeur d'Alene district miners a thrill when he flew this Curtiss pusher at a Kellogg picnic August 16, 1913.

"For the first time in the history of the Coeur d'Alenes an aeroplane ascended yesterday, not once, but twice, and the 7,000 people who were in attendance at the tenth annual picnic of the Wardner Industrial Union saw two of the most perfect flights that were ever witnessed." Frank Bryant made those flights at Kellogg on August 16, 1913, wearing a black mourning band on his sleeve in memory of his brother Johnny, killed only ten days earlier while flying a hydroplane at Victoria.[47]

T.T. Maroney of Montana also flew at Kellogg that day but had engine trouble and

ISHS 79-141.38/d

Above: T.T. Maroney barely made this takeoff over some stumps at Kellogg on August 16, 1913 -- the same day Frank Bryant flew. Minutes later his engine died and he crashed. See photo opposite.

Right, top: T.T. Maroney survived his Kellogg crash August 16, 1913.

Right, bottom: Glenn Curtiss publicity photos were used to promote company pilots. We have no record of J.C. Mars flying in Idaho, but the photo clearly shows the hazard to the pilot of the engine placement.

made a crash landing on a hillside covered with rocks and stumps. He saved his life "by letting the aeroplane land where it would and climbing upon the engine for safety as it went up against the hill." The Curtiss biplane, property of the McClelland Aviation company, was a total loss except for the engine.[48]

Blackfoot failed to get a flying exhibition at its 1913 fair, when the contracting company failed to show, and had an equally frustrating experience in 1914. In a comedy of errors that few local people found amusing, the fair directors actually had two planes in town for awhile and two contracts, but got only one short flight and a lot of grief from the outfit that did fly. The flier's manager demanded advance payment before attempting a second flight, then refused to allow the pilot to fly at all when it became clear that the contract called for payment of $200 only after each flight was completed. Upon threat of a law suit, and an attachment on the plane, the pilot started a takeoff and ran into two fence posts, making the plane inoperable. In the heat of the altercation that followed the fair board accused the pilot of deliberately

ISHS 79-141.38/e

wrecking the plane to keep from fulfilling the contract.[49]

Boise's Fourth of July flying exhibition in 1916 had a timely twist due to Pancho Villa's attack on Columbus, New Mexico, March 8 and 9. In addition to the by now standard race between a plane and a racing car, companies H and D of the Idaho National Guard took part in a battle with a "Mexican aviator." The flier was O.E. Williams, and as he swooped low over the fairgrounds infield, tossing out "bombs" that exploded in mid-air, he was fired at "fusillade after fusillade" by the ground troops. "The big biplane, figuratively riddled with bullets, was soon brought to the earth and its pilot captured, to be paraded in front of the grandstand."[50] Three days later the guardsmen left Boise for Arizona and the Mexican border "with songs on their lips and smiles in their eyes," to support General John J. Pershing and the regulars, then 400 miles into Mexico chasing Villa and his guerillas.[51] In a few more months, after America entered the Great War, the Idaho boys were on their way to France and the Western Front.

Other events of that July 4, 1916, meet were a three mile race between a plane and a racecar driven by Mrs. F.A. Nelson, which she won by the length of the car's hood. An attempt to deliver Boise's first airmail between the fairgrounds and the downtown post office failed when pilot Al Boshek's motor "unaccountably stopped" just as he cleared the ground. The plane nosedived into the turf, scattering the specially printed souvenir mail all over the field. Postmaster P.M. Davis conscientiously had all of the cards picked up, even those shredded by the airplane's propeller. They were pasted together and mailed as promised, even though their time as "airmail" could be reckoned in seconds.[52]

ISHS 79-141.38/a

Courtesy National Archives

Lt. H.W. Puryear, left, with the German Fokker D-7 that he flew in Boise with the Victory Loan Flying Circus, April 19, 1919. His mechanics had assembled it moments before.

Courtesy National Archives

Another crew of Army mechanics, posed with their Lieutenant, right, had just unpacked their Curtiss Jenny from the baggage cars in the background and assembled it for flying in Boise.

ISHS 70-85.15

One of the British S.E. 5s that flew in Boise on April 19, 1919.

FLYING CIRCUS

III

One of the most exciting days in southwest Idaho history came on April 19, 1919, when a "flying circus" came to Boise. There had been aviation meets and barnstorming fliers in town before, but this group was different.

The planes were fighters from the first World War that had ended on November 11 the year before. They were in Idaho to put on an aerial reenactment of the dogfights over the Western Front that had made combat pilots the glamour boys of a grisly, gray trench war that cost millions of lives and was singularly lacking in glamour otherwise.

The purpose of the big show, billed as the Victory Flying Circus, was to sell war bonds at stops in major cities throughout the West. There had been four Liberty Loan drives during the war, and this, the fifth, was called the Victory Loan drive. In all, the effort raised 21 billion dollars to help pay for America's part in World War I.[1]

A special train pulled into town at 6:30 a.m., and was switched to the Barber spur to get as close to the polo grounds at Boise Barracks as possible. The planes were packed into specially remodeled railway cars in disassembled form, but could be put back together in a hurry by 11 crews of four men each. Typically, 11 planes were flown at each location, out of a total of 19 carried. In addition to the wings and fuselages, packed separately, there were plenty of spare parts for all of the planes.[2]

A roster of the ships carried by the flying circus listed five American Curtiss JN-4 "Jennies," four British S.E. 5s, four French Spads and five German Fokkers. In Boise that day, all of the Jennies flew, along with two Fokkers, two S.E. 5s, and one Spad. A total of nine hours of flying time was logged and seven civilian passengers were given rides. This was more time and more passengers than the circus recorded at any of its other stops throughout the far West.[3]

Noteworthy among the passengers was Idaho Governor D.W. Davis, who had earlier taken a short ride when the circus visited Pocatello on April 18.[4] This time he flew for a full half hour, and had his mettle tested at the end when his pilot, Lt. Henry W. Webb, looped his plane at 4,000 feet, and then went into a tailspin of 1,700 feet. The Governor told the crowd gathered round after the landing that it was "a great sensation."[5]

The Victory Loan flying circus attracted more than 50,000 people to Boise. They came from eastern Oregon, Caldwell, Nampa and every other town in southwest Idaho. The *Statesman* called it the "greatest crowd ever seen here," and it surely must have been. A feature of the day of flying by the World War I fighting planes was that there were no accidents, but the greatest hazard seems to have been encountered by the motorists who jammed Boise streets. "Drivers had a difficult time," said the paper, "for many of them could not take their eyes off the fascinating machines to watch the road." Extra policemen put on that day estimated that there were 3,000 out-of-town autos crowding the city's streets.[6]

What the crowds saw, in addition to simulated aerial combat between German Fokker fighters and allied planes, was formation flying "in V and echelon," and "loops, barrel rolls, spiral nose dives, tail spins and stalls." The two German planes were flown by Major Carl Spaatz, commander of the circus, and by 1st Lt. H.W. Puryear who had achieved a certain fame

Courtesy National Archives

Courtesy National Archives

Courtesy National Archives

Top left: People lined up three deep around Boise's polo grounds on April 19, 1919, to see Captain Carl Spaatz and his flying circus.

Top right: At the request of Governor D.W. Davis a Curtiss Jenny was flown to Arrowrock Dam to take this photo.

Above: The wings of Idaho's capitol building were still under construction when this view of downtown was taken April 19, 1919.

during the war by escaping from a German prisoner of war camp.[7]

One of the Curtiss Jennies flew to Arrow Rock dam and back at the request of Governor Davis in order to take photographs of what was then the largest dam in the world. A series of other aerial photos of Boise and vicinity was taken that day. "Aerial photography requires nervy operators," explained the *Statesman*, "for the photographer must stand up in the fuselage in order to snap the ground beneath. For a time it was feared that the plane would not be able to fly to the dam, as the mountains create air currents which form pockets or 'bumps' and make flying, especially photography, difficult, as a plane will sometimes fall 1,000 feet when it enters one of these pockets."[8]

Two Boise women were among those brave enough to fly with the army pilots. They were Mrs. C.C. Anderson, chairman of the city's Red Cross chapter, and Mrs. Sam Ballantyne, also active in Red Cross work. Mrs. Joseph A. Partridge of Nampa also flew. Governor Davis spent 30 minutes in the air, and Ed Peasley, local committeeman for the event, was also honored with a flight.[9]

For the thousands from out of town who came to Boise for the flying circus, the experience was thrilling, but something of a physical ordeal as well. Nine-year-old David Dorsey remembered it vividly 72 years later. The trip by Model T Ford from Sunny Slope, west of Caldwell, started at 6:00 a.m. when neighbors gathered at the Dorsey place to form an automobile caravan headed for Boise. The wagon road they followed for over 30 miles was rutted

Left to right: A French Spad and two British S.E. 5 fighters. The irrigation ditch in foreground bordered the polo grounds field.

ISHS 71-122.11

and dusty. At Collister, asphalt paving was encountered for the first time. At noon hundreds of families had pulled off the road to eat the picnics the mothers had prepared. It was "a quick lunch," Dorsey recalled, "for two reasons: number one, the terrible dust, and number two, there were aeroplanes buzzing over Boise. That was what we had come to see, and we were a long way from the site of the show."

To the excited and impatient children in the little group, it seemed they would never get to the polo grounds. When the jam of cars forced a halt, everybody got out and walked the last mile and a half, and once there at last, "the only way we kids could see anything except butts was to have our folks lift us up above their shoulders." The men took turns holding up the children, but the little ones cried most of the time. "To say the least, it was a very trying experience." There was more discomfort to come. "We were there possibly one hour. When we left, the kids and a lot of papas and mamas needed to find a bush, and there were no bushes. I have forgotten how this came out, but it wasn't good. Neither the show nor the city dads had made provision for needs of nature."

When the little caravan got back to Sunny Slope it was about 9:00 p.m., and all of the usual farm chores still had to be done, feeding livestock, milking the cows, and separating the milk . . . "I was about as tired as any kid could get in a day."[10]

In their official report, now preserved in the National Archives, the circus officers made no mention of sanitary facilities, but praised Boise's efforts to make the exhibition a success. Cooperation was "very good" and "all arrangements very satisfactory." It was also noted that Governor Davis had given the circus his "personal attention," and that the event was unusually well advertised. (By contrast, Los Angeles had received "poor marks" for both cooperation and advertising).

The report also gives a good description of Boise's polo field which served as an airport that day. (Boise Little Theater and Boise Senior Center are two present buildings on the site). The field, said the account, was "level and smooth, 2,000 feet long and 1,600 feet wide. Surrounded on two sides with irrigation ditch and two sides with barbed fence."[11] By comparison with this 2,000 foot strip, Boise's 1926 field was soon abandoned because its 3,600 foot runway was too short to be safe.

Major Carl Spaatz, Executive Officer of the circus, had won the Distinguished Service Cross while flying with the 13th Aero Squadron on the Western Front. He shot down three German planes. "Tooey" Spaatz would go on to make aviation history in the second World War. In 1941 he was Chief of Staff to General Hap Arnold. In July, 1942, he was given command of all U.S. air forces in the European Theater of Operations, then made Commander of the 12th Air Force, and in 1943 took over the entire strategic bombing operation against Germany. He represented the U.S. at the Berlin surrender of May 8, 1945, and was then put in charge of the B-29 raids against Japan that ended the war in the Pacific. Spaatz is often considered the father of the Air Force as a separate branch of the service, on par with the Army and Navy, since his testimony to Congress helped bring it about in 1947.[12]

Courtesy Don Duvall

This barnstorming Curtiss Jenny attracted a crowd when it landed at the Boise polo field in the early Twenties.

ISHS 77-139.42

Crowds gathered around this barnstormer near Kimberly. Many took their first airplane ride that day.

ISHS MS 247

Young Basil "Bake" Russell sent this snapshot of himself in a Fokker D-7 to his mother in the late Twenties. He and older brother Joe grew up in Payette. Basil was killed in 1930 in Los Angeles when the passenger liner he was piloting crashed and burned.

BARNSTORMERS AND DAREDEVILS IV

They landed in cow pastures and stubblefields, slept in haystacks, or on the ground under the wings of their planes. They battled dust and dogs, coughing engines, and stormy weather. They risked their necks every day, yet wouldn't have changed places with anyone else on earth. They were the barnstormers.

When the first World War ended in 1918, and Uncle Sam began rapid demobilization of the armed forces, there were several thousand young aviators who had learned to fly at government expense and had acquired a love of adventure in the sky.

Fortunately for them, the army began to declare surplus thousands of aircraft that had been built during 1917 and 1918, and made them available for a few hundred dollars apiece. Most numerous of these was the Curtiss JN-4 "Jenny," with its reliable OX-5 engine. In this plane most American military pilots had learned to fly. The other old standby of the flying service during the war was the De Havilland DH-4, and a lot of those became available too. Throughout the 1920s and into the 1930s, these two models were flown everywhere in America in flying circuses and daredevil barnstorming exhibitions.

For young men and women who wanted to keep on flying after the war, or to take it up, an early step was usually to acquire a surplus JN-4 or DH-4, either by themselves or in partnership with others. Then, to support a hobby that for most became a compulsion, the young fliers took to barnstorming.

The term "barnstorming" came into use in the late 19th Century. It was first used by touring theatrical companies to describe performing in rural districts, and then by politicians campaigning for the country vote.[1] For fliers, traveling through rural areas where there were still millions of Americans who had never seen an airplane, and many brave enough to fly in one if given the chance, barnstorming presented pilots a way to make money doing what they loved best.[2]

Although many small towns in Idaho had seen planes fly in the 'teens, those had been short exhibition flights of a few minutes each. In the 1920s, using Jennies and De Havillands, pilots offered a much more varied program. Typically, the first part of the show was exhibition flying, like that presented at Shoshone on April 24, 1920, with "all the stunts known, including the Himmelman (sic) turn, the barrel roll, loop the loop, etc."[3] Next, pilot Hugh Barker took passengers for short flights, and since most biplanes used in barnstorming could take two passengers in the forward cockpit, the flier could make what was then a lot of money in one day. It was the aerial acrobatics that drew the crowds, after which the more daring lined up for a flight.

Hugh Barker had flown at Pocatello and Burley that spring, and carried Idaho's first authorized air mail from Pocatello to Idaho Falls on April 15, 1920. J. Robb Brady received permission from the U.S. Postal department to make the flight in early April, and Barker made the trip to Idaho Falls and back in time to take up some paying passengers at Pocatello for short sightseeing flights.[4]

There were no licensed airports in Idaho in 1920, but there was increasing interest in building them. The Idaho Auto & Aeroplane Co. of Boise negotiated with Boise Independent School District for land it owned near the city auto camp grounds, for permission to build

ISHS 66-14.2

Nick Mamer and Clyde Pangborn flew this water-cooled Jenny on a forest fire spotting mission near Bovill in 1922. Both were Army Reserve officers at the time.

a landing strip. "Should the deal go through, this station will be listed with the Aero Club of America and with the government and all flyers making transcontinental or trans-state trips would make it a regular stopping place . . . it would give both the autoist and the flyer a common camping place."[5]

In May, an "Aero Club of Idaho" was formed at a meeting of Boise Chamber of Commerce for the express purpose of seeing that a municipal airport was established, but it would take nearly six more years to get the job done. Meanwhile, visiting pilots and barnstormers continued to land at the polo grounds, fairgrounds, or in farmers' fields near the city.[6]

The Idaho State Fair of 1920 featured airplane flights and stunts by Nick Mamer of Spokane and his daredevil mechanic E.E. Tatterfield. The two had performed at Portland and other northwest cities earlier. In addition to a contract paying them for their appearance and acrobatic performance, they had a chance to make more money by giving passenger rides. It was Tatterfield's performance that wowed them at Boise in 1920:

"Hanging in mid air from his plane with one hand, thousands of feet above the grounds, E.E. Tatterfield performed antics which inspired the crowds with awe. His plane almost in the clouds, he walked along its wings, crawled under its wheels, and hung by his legs. And then, as if his stunts were not enough to satisfy the audience, he flew upside down and on the side, did nosedives and long spiral dives." Of course, it was Nick Mamer at the controls and Tatterfield risking his neck on the outside of the plane, although the reporter momentarily thought of it as a one man show.[7]

As usual, there was a race between Mamer's plane and an auto supplied by a local dealer, even though by 1920 this was more of a tradition than a real contest. The car had the distinct advantage because the plane's actual speed was negated by the wide turns it was forced to make.[8] During one of his trips with a passenger, Mamer's plane hit a ditch on takeoff. It slowed him up enough that he decided to go under, rather than over, some telephone lines at the edge of the field. He cleared those, but snagged the trolley lines of the streetcar system and crashed. He and his passenger were unhurt, but the plane was damaged badly enough that repairs could not be made in time for a scheduled appearance at Weiser.[9]

The nation's death toll from automobile accidents was rising at an alarming rate in the 1920s, and it was a car crash in Nebraska that took the life of Volara Romanza Nelson, an Idaho woman who was reportedly the first female pilot licensed by the Aero Club of America. When she lived in Boise, Mrs. Nelson managed an automobile agency. Earlier, Rupert had been her home. At the time of her death July 2, 1921, she was 32, and had been barnstorming throughout the central states.[10]

One of the greatest and best known of all the stunt fliers and teachers in the Pacific Northwest was Tex Rankin. On October 1, 1921, Tex and his partner Ralph Beal landed at the polo grounds in their Curtiss Skylark. Next day, they performed one acrobatic flight before taking up passengers. No less than 53 Boiseans flew on Sunday, October 2, and with business that good, Rankin and Beal decided to stay over another day before flying to an engagement at the Weiser Roundup.[11]

Barnstormers of those days occasionally picked up business passengers too. On October 4, 1921, officials of Mountain States Telephone Co. chartered Tex Rankin to fly them to Weiser with passes over Nampa and Caldwell on the way. Since Weiser, like most towns, had no airfield, "fully 15 minutes was lost circling about . . . to find a proper landing field."[12] Even with the slow landing speeds of those early biplanes, a rough field often caused flip-ups and broken propellers. Planes were damaged more often than pilots on such occasions, and most old-timer barnstormers who survived could tell tales of walking away from several such wrecks.

Pilot Ray Black of California flew his French Hispano-Suiza biplane into Boise in October, 1921, and found the city "a jinx." In taking off from the polo grounds field a wheel collapsed in soft sand, flipping the plane and breaking the propeller. After repairs, a second trial led to a worse disaster. Insufficient power on takeoff led the pilot to attempt too steep an ascent, he stalled and caught a treetop with the tail. The plane, spun around by other trees, then crashed,

ISHS MS 247

Joe Russell of Payette in his first plane -- a JN4D that he traded a Ford car and $800 for. He barnstormed out of Ontario, Oregon, in the 1930s and later had a long career as an airline pilot in South America.

narrowly missing the house of Leo J. Falk, prominent Boise businessman. Only about half of the $6,700 plane was salvageable.[13]

Don Jokisch, a local barnstormer who had performed in southern Idaho and Utah towns, was testing a homemade monoplane near Cole School on May 23, 1924, when he nosedived into a cowshed and was killed instantly. He had survived an earlier crash at the Grandview, Idaho, fair in October, 1923, but his woman passenger from Glenns Ferry, riding in the forward cockpit, was killed. Jokisch, badly shaken, but only slightly injured, told reporters, "I have had some close calls, but never so close as this one was. I sure thought I was 'going west' on that trip."[14] In less than a year he would take his fatal plunge.

A new twist was given to barnstorming in 1925 when a plane was sent across the state to publicize the dedication of the big dam then being built across Snake River at American Falls. Dubbed the *Dam Eagle,* the plane flew from Ashton to Weiser with several stops along the way. It was an appropriate way to sell the American Falls celebration, since "an unusual aerial exhibition" was a feature of the event. Thousands of leaflets were dropped over towns along the route, reading "Meeting the fliers at American Falls on July 13." *Dam Eagle,* piloted by Capt. Hubbard Seeley, Army Air Corps Reserve, was invited to stay over in Nampa to take part in a "sham battle" with artillery, machine guns and a tank, all pretending to attack "the Hindenburg Line."[15]

Nick Mamer of Spokane, who barnstormed often in Idaho in the Twenties, got into more of a sham battle than he bargained for at Moscow on October 16, 1925. He had been hired by Washington State College students to help them set fire to the University of Idaho's bonfire. It was intended to be lit that night on the eve of the big football game between the two Palouse schools. The plan was to drop phosphorous "bombs" on the big pile of flammables and burn it up prematurely. Although pilot Mamer zoomed over the bonfire several times at a level of only ten feet, watchful Vandal students raked the bombs out of the pile before they could get it burning. An unexpected ally of the students was Latah County Sheriff Charles

ISHS 76-216.3

Charles T. Wrightson, Varney Air Lines manager in Boise in 1926, began his aviation career as a barnstormer with a Curtiss Jenny. This photo is dated 1924.

Summerfield who peppered the plane with birdshot to warn it away.[16]

Nampa staged its biggest flying circus to that time, when it celebrated the opening of the Pacific Fruit Express shops in 1926. The shops, a complement to Nampa's railroad industry, were of great economic importance to the town for many years, building, repairing, and servicing refrigerator cars. Robert McLaghtin, former Royal Flying Corps pilot, and Van R. Osdale, a U.S. Army reserve office, were booked to perform aerial stunts, parachute jumps and "straight flying."[17]

Teaching others to fly offered another way for barnstormers to eke out a living. A few, like Art Walters of Baker, Oregon, settled down and started schools. Walters, a war hero decorated by General John J. Pershing, was in Boise in 1926 taking any flying work he could get. He flew one airmail trip for Varney Air Lines from Boise to Pasco on April 7, the day after the service was inaugurated, using one of the newly assembled Swallow biplanes.[18] A few days later he decided to locate in Boise and start a flying school, saying that the enthusiasm the town

Courtesy Malcolm Parsons estate

Unidentified early barnstormers somewhere in Idaho.

Courtesy Dan Stohr

Above: Young Penn Stohr posed proudly with his first airplane. He, like most young pilots of the Twenties, made expenses by barnstorming. Stohr was later a noted mountain pilot for Johnson Flying Service.

Top right: An unidentified early southern Idaho barnstormer with his Jenny. Note the S-curved wooden propeller and the heavy leather flying coat.

had shown for flying at the big Airmail Festival April 6 had convinced him that there were plenty of potential students awaiting instruction.[19] On May 1 he flew in from Portland with a Curtiss Jenny to be used as a trainer, and also shipped in a damaged Jenny that had cracked up on the coast for use in a course on mechanics and repair. He soon had a dozen eager students and began advertising "passenger and cross country flights" in the newspapers.[20]

In 1927 Walters and Virgil Adair, another old barnstormer, who had been flying since 1920, worked as instructors in what was now Southern Idaho Airways, Inc. An ad announcing the start of a new class appeared on September 10, with a picture of *The Spirit of St. Louis.* Since Lindbergh had appeared in Boise less than a week before, this was a timely way to take advantage of the city's keen interest in flying.[21] Adair's beginning with his new employer was hardly auspicious. On September 11 he smashed the company's pride and joy, a Waco Ten, while attempting a takeoff from the municipal airport. The low telephone wires at the Broadway Avenue end of the field, a constant hazard to all fliers at the time, caused him to climb too steeply, lose speed, and pancake into big cottonwood trees. He and his two passengers were unhurt, but the plane was badly damaged. An eyewitness said "Mr. Adair, heading into a strong gust of wind, did noble work, but the top of that old cottonwood fouled his plane." Even old barnstormers could come to grief on supposedly routine flights with passengers.[22]

Adair's crash caused Boise's mayor to declare that there would be no recurrence of such mishaps. It was recalled that the great Charles Lindbergh had advised city officials to "cut down all trees around your airport," only a few weeks earlier, and now it was done.[23] Adair, continuing his barnstorming at Weiser and Cambridge, Idaho, fairs, had one forced landing due to engine trouble, but this time no damage was done to the plane.[24] Forced landings were routine, for a variety of reasons, including sudden changes in the weather, shortage of fuel, and the fall of darkness.

The passengers who rode with the early barnstormers were of all ages, occupations and

ISHS 61-143.77

temperaments. The kind that made feature stories for the newspapers were usually the very old or the very young. "Pioneer Mother Delighted With Airplane Ride" was the headline of a story describing a flight taken in Boise on August 27, 1927. Mrs. Sarah DeHaven Stucker had crossed the plains in a covered wagon in 1859, and was 88 when she went for a spin with Harry O. McDougall, a much decorated World War I fighter pilot who had continued to fly after he became an assistant Idaho Attorney General.[25] It was McDougall who flew former Idaho Chief Justice Isaac Sullivan earlier that year when the judge was 79.[26] McDougall would be killed at Pocatello on Armistice Day, 1928, while in a race sponsored by the American Legion. With him when his Monocoupe crashed was his 20-year-old sister-in-law on her first and last flight.[27]

J. Howard Firebaugh, later of Mountain Home, related what were rather typical experiences from his own barnstorming years between 1929 and 1931: "On a good day you could take 40 or 50 flights. At five dollars a flight, or two and a half for each passenger, that wasn't bad. Gas didn't cost so much in those days and living expenses, even on the road, didn't cost too much." Of his passengers he recalled "We'd fly them over their house or farm. Most of them just wanted to feel what it was like . . . and there were a number of things one could do with that aircraft to give passengers a thrill. Only once in a while would disappointed passengers demand their money back, and only once in a while were they glad to get out.[28]

Early Curtiss pilot Charley Willard once told of his closest call while barnstorming. He was flying in Oklahoma when the weather turned so bad he was forced to call off further flights that day. The crowd was very disappointed and one "big native" pulled a gun and told the flier, "You might as well go up and take your chances because if you don't I'll kill you right here." Willard flew, but wrecked his plane and was lucky to come out alive.[29]

Tex Rankin was back in Idaho in 1928, this time with a Ryan Brougham, sister ship of Lindbergh's famous *Spirit of St. Louis.*" Art Walters was his assistant. The two gave rides to 150 people on May 6 at a meet sponsored by

ISHS 76-216.5

Boise Flying Club members posed proudly in 1928 with the club's new Hisso-American. There were four women members in the group. The club's brown bear mascot, far left, sometimes flew, but usually got airsick and made a mess.

the Boise Flying Club.[30] September 30 that year the club used the occasion of turning on the new landing lights at Boise's airport to put on another flying meet, hoping to raise enough money from admissions to buy a training plane for its members. This time Varney airmail pilots Leon Cuddeback, Paul Andert and George Buck competed in the stunt flying event with Tommy Thompson of Salt Lake City. Although Thompson won the prize, many thought Paul Andert, the mail pilot, had done better. William Gowen, brother of Paul Gowen, for whom the Boise Air Corps base would later be named, drew special praise for flying at night with fireworks decorating his plane.[31] Ralph Sharpnak, another Salt Lake City pilot, was in town a week later. He carried 327 Boise passengers as part of a barnstorming circuit that included flights at Idaho Falls, Pocatello, Burley and Twin Falls.[32]

In 1930 "Wild Irish" Bill Haddock brought his daredevil act to southern Idaho. He had made more than 1,200 parachute jumps and was noted for wing walking and gymnastics on a trapeze suspended from a speeding plane. Six ships took part in the flying circus he presented September 7, 1930, at Boise municipal field. Virgil Adair was one of those who did stunt flying that day. Advance publicity was colorful, and would have done credit to P.T. Barnum: "Boise's Greatest Flying Circus, Bigger and Better, The World's Greatest Airplane Trapeze Performer — he performs hair-raising stunts . . . hangs by his teeth while at an altitude of 2,000 feet in the air . . . he will hold you spellbound." Haddock's Travelair monoplane was billed as "the largest airplane ever to be stunted in Boise." The daredevil came to Idaho from Montana after performing a week earlier at the Chicago air races. Haddock had also doubled for Hollywood actors in several aviation movies.[33]

When San Diego pilot and stunt man Jack "Buddy" Bruce came to southwest Idaho in March, 1931, local fliers organized an impromptu circus to back his parachuting exhibitions. Bruce had made some spectacular plane crashes for the Hollywood movie hit of 1930, *Hell's Angels,* but was now barnstorming with his 'chute. Virgil Adair, Lionel Kay, Jack Dawne, Bob King, and Cliff Bennett all stunted over Boise airport at Bruce's first appearance, while a crowd of 1,000 looked on.[34]

So successful was this March 1 show that it was repeated several times, with Bruce attracting lots of press. He landed hard at Nampa on April 11 when the air went out of his 'chute 100 feet above the ground. He was knocked out, but suffered only a sprained ankle and a lot of bruises. A Nampa farmer, in whose field Bruce landed, said he bounced hard three times. "I thought he was a goner."[35] Far from being a goner, Buddy Bruce jumped over Boise next day from 13,750 feet, did a free fall of 2,520, then landed in trees in a downtown alley. He was unhurt, but the fire department had to rescue his parachute. He went on to American Falls, Idaho Falls and Pocatello on his barnstorming trip.[36]

Jack Dawne, who had flown in the aerial circuses over Boise with Buddy Bruce, was killed at Payette's annual Apple Blossom Festival on May 1, 1931. The "survivor of many thrilling escapades of recent years . . . was hurled to instant death before thousands of horror-stricken witnesses" when his De Havilland Moth nose-dived into the ground from 100 feet up. Pilot error was blamed for the tragedy, the verdict of most being that he had been stunting too low and didn't realize how close he was to the ground.[37]

The Northwest Pacific States Air Tour came to Nampa on June 29, 1931. Famous stunt pilot Tex Rankin headed the cast of a show that featured 46 planes and a group of women daredevils. Dorothy Hester, who had learned to fly with Rankin at Portland, was billed as "the premier woman stunt flier in the world." She held the women's world record with 63 outside loops. (Rankin held the men's record of 76.) Her specialty was upside-down flying, and her 56 consecutive upside-down rolls was most by either men or women at the time. Jackie Brown, 17-year-old Los Angeles girl, parachuted, as did her older sister Billy, who had jumped from a plane more times than any other woman in the world.

Nick Mamer of Spokane brought the largest plane to the meet, a Ford Trimotor, and the smallest, a Bull Pup. All of the visiting fliers were guests at a banquet in the famous Dewey Palace Hotel, hosted by the Nampa Chamber of Commerce. Baker, Oregon, was the next stop of the touring aviators when they left Idaho on the morning of June 30, 1931.[38]

By the end of the 1930s, organized air shows had largely replaced the barnstormers of early days. Level and fairly smooth airfields in most larger Idaho towns, equipped with hangars, lighting, and radio communications had replaced the cow pastures, farmers' fields and sagebrush where the pioneers had bumped in to do their stuff. By then, most small Idaho towns had some kind of landing strip,[39] and at least one resident pilot. True, they still gave rides to passengers, and flying lessons to support their hobby, but more and more commercial opportunities were opening up. Many in Idaho became bush pilots, ferrying mail, passengers and supplies to remote mountain areas.

One early barnstormer from Idaho, Clyde Pangborn, brought his first plane, a Curtiss Jenny, to his home town of St. Maries in 1918.[40] He had learned to fly in the Aviation Section of the Army Signal Corps, and like many young fliers of the era took to barnstorming. At Ashland, Oregon, in 1921 Pangborn met Van Gates with whom he joined company as a member of Gates Flying Circus, the most famous barnstorming troup of the 1920s and early '30s. Pangborn was soon the star of this gang of daredevils, performing before more than 50 million people all over America. He became noted as "Upside Down Pangborn" for his specialty, but also did wing walking and the other crowd thrillers for which the circus became famous.[41]

In 1931 he teamed with Hugh Herndon, Jr., to achieve international acclaim and a place in aviation history when they made the first non-stop crossing of the Pacific Ocean from Japan to Washington state. Pangborn had planned to end the record flight in Boise, but was forced by fog to turn back to Wenatchee. His landing there on October 5, 1931, gave the crowds gathered a thrill, for the plane had no wheels. In order to reduce wind resistance for the long flight, a special detachable landing gear had been installed in Tokyo. It was cut loose shortly after takeoff, but when not all of it fell, Clyde Pangborn crawled out of the cabin and along a wing strut to pry it loose. At Wenatchee he made a safe pancake landing in a cloud of dust, just 41 hours after takeoff.[42]

Courtesy Wayne White

Tex Rankin of Portland was the greatest stunt pilot in the Pacific Northwest for a generation. He posed with Florence Krall (in the cockpit) at Boise in 1931 with his new Great Lakes. He died years later in a crash.

ISHS 72-190.50/b

Two great stunt fliers in one picture: Laura Ingalls and Tex Rankin, Boise, 1938.

FLYING THE MAIL

V

Regular airmail service in the United States was begun between New York and Washington, D.C., on May 15, 1918, as a joint operation of the War and Post Office Departments. It was taken over and greatly expanded by the Post Office between August 12, 1918, and 1926, when contracts were let to private business. Idaho's significant moment in airmail history came then, when Varney Air Lines began flying commercial airmail on the Pasco-Boise-Elko route.

During the years when the Post Office flew the mail, some progress was made in speed, efficiency and expanded routes, but with the planes and facilities of those days it was always dangerous. Army pilots and De Havilland 4 Army biplanes, remodeled to carry mail in their forward cockpits, were used until wartime demands for men and machines forced the Department to acquire its own small fleet of DH-4s and hire civilian pilots. At first the mail was flown only in daylight and transferred to trains for the night segments of the routes. By train alone it had taken 91 hours for a letter to cross the country. The train-plane combination reduced the time to 57 hours in winter and 54 hours in summer.[1] Weather, always a variable, sometimes disrupted the schedule, but with no beacon lights, lighted airfields or radio communication, flying both day and night by plane was next to impossible.

On routes where it was first tried, even daylight flying was suicidally dangerous. The one from New York to Chicago was deadly in winter. Of the 40 original pilots on that route, 30 were killed flying the mail within a few years. Flying the Cleveland-New York segment alone, over the Allegheny Mountains, two died in 1919, five in 1920, and 12 in 1921.[2] No wonder the airmail pioneers called their DH-4s "flying bricks," but it wasn't so much the fault of the planes as it was the Post Office's traditional insistence that "The Mail Must Go Through," no matter what the weather.

Mail was flown between Pocatello and Idaho Falls briefly in 1920, under special authorization from the Post Office, but with the proviso that it be "without cost to the government."[3] The transcontinental route, New York to San Francisco, opened that year, and Idaho, like most of the country without air access to it, tried to get a connection.

The one most favored by Idaho was Seattle-Boise-Salt Lake, but Spokane also wanted a link to Salt Lake via Boise. Not until 1925, however, could Idaho become optimistic about receiving airmail service. On February 22, 1925, Congress passed the Kelly Bill, authorizing the Post Office to award airmail contracts to private companies. The Pasco-Boise-Elko route was the one selected to connect the Northwest with the San Francisco-New York run.

On October 27, 1925, Walter T. Varney, who operated a flying school at San Mateo, California, was awarded what had been designated Contract Air Mail 5 (C.A.M. 5). Varney had shrewdly guessed that his best chance of getting a contract was to choose one that few others would want — the difficult mountain and desert "sagebrush route," Pasco-Boise-Elko. There were no other bidders. Since passengers were not expected on a line that connected these three small and isolated communities, Varney could use small planes much like those used in his flying school. He could also man his little air line with his own instructors and mechanics. It was because of these initial advantages that Varney was able to fly the first airmail in the west under Kelly Bill contract. He ordered six Swallow open cockpit biplanes fitted with

ISHS 77-14.44

Varney Air Lines' fleet of new Swallows lined up in Boise, spring, 1926. Only the ship at far right had not had its 90 h.p. in-line engine replaced with a 150 h.p. Wright Whirlwind radial.

Leon D. Cuddeback, Walter Varney's chief pilot, who made the historic first contract airmail flight on April 6, 1926.

90-horsepower in-line engines, and sent Chief Pilot Leon D. Cuddeback to prepare facilities at the three towns.[4]

There was much to be done before the planes arrived in Boise, where company headquarters would be located. The first task was to secure decent landing facilities in the three towns to be served. Boise, which had been using the Polo Grounds at Boise Barracks as a landing field for half a dozen years, or the fairgrounds oval for exhibition flights, had long been aware that it needed a municipal field with better facilities. The Chamber of Commerce regularly received inquiries from out of state asking about flying services available in Idaho's capital. As early as 1920 a committee of the Chamber discussed ways and means of acquiring a site for an air field, and an anonymous private donor said he would give the land when the city was ready.[5] When J.A. Fennell wrote a feature story in 1921, predicting what Boise would be like in 50 years, he said the city would have "a well-kept aviation field on the bench," and that "individual ownership of airplanes" would be common. "Definite air traffic rules and regulations will be in place, and zoning systems to provide the means for policing."

ISHS 76-40.2/a

Fennell was right on target with these predictions, but had too much faith in the future of dirigibles. He thought Boise's bench airport would have "hourly dirigible balloon service to eastern centers and to the western coasts. Boise will have met this development with a great landing field, with anchoring towers and huge hangar stations." In 1921 nobody could have predicted the series of dirigible disasters that would cause nearly total abandonment of their further development or use.[6]

The "great landing field" on the bench would be in place in 1971, as predicted, but on the Whitney Bench, far south of the location Fennell had in mind. The city's immediate need for a field to accommodate Walter Varney's airmail finally led to the choice of a location nobody had thought of in 1921, on the south side of the Boise River where Boise State University is today. But it was a struggle getting the site chosen and the field built. Cyril C. Thompson, Commander of Boise's John Regan post of the American Legion, was in the center of the successful effort to overcome the many difficulties. He later recalled that Walter T. Varney and his chief pilot, Leon Cuddeback, both war veterans, had joined the Boise post and made many friends there. When they mentioned that the company was getting discouraged at the lack of progress toward selecting a site and building a field, and might have to give up its contract and go back to running the San Mateo flying school, Thompson decided to take emergency action. He called on Mayor Ern G. Eagleson who told him that the city was in a very unhappy situation because of all the political pressure it was getting to buy land for the field from a number of powerful business interests, including the city's largest bank. Most sites offered were not acceptable to fliers, chiefly because they were too small or too close to the foothills or other obstruction.[7]

The solution proposed by Cyril Thompson was to use a piece of land the city already owned on the south side of Boise River — an undeveloped tract that had been donated for future expansion of Julia Davis Park. The mayor doubted that it could ever be made into an airfield, because "it was a wild 40 acres of willow clumps, brush, trees and flood washouts." Once known as Ridenbaugh's Island, since a south branch of the Boise River en-

Courtesy Chet Moulton

Boise's riverside airport was under construction when this winter aerial view was taken in 1926. Broadway Avenue is in the foreground.

Walter Varney, left, stands in front of one of the newly arrived Swallows with its 90 h.p. Curtiss water-cooled engine. The identity of the two men at right, standing beside the big Packard, has been lost.

circled it at the base of the bench, the future airport was underlaid with rounded river cobbles of all sizes, and had very little topsoil.

The volunteers who cleared the rocky site for Boise's new airport were led by members of the American Legion post and its 40 et 8 Club. Thompson challenged his Legionnaires "to perform an airport miracle" and to show the same spirit some of them had shown near Chateau-Thierry, France, in 1918 when they cleared the way for artillery and supply trains on their way to the front. The city's Rotary, Kiwanis, Exchange and Ad Clubs also pitched in. On February 18 it was announced that the volunteers would gather at Broadway bridge and "advance as skirmishers with grubbing hoes and axes through the willows of the 40 acre tract." The first assault was to clear a path 300 feet wide for a runway that could then be leveled by six teams of men and horses using plows and fresnos. A city-owned road grader was also put to work, and a tractor pulled trees too big to be grubbed out by hand.[8]

Adding to the festive character of the occasion was the American Legion's 40 et 8 band. Members rode around on a truck, serenading the workers. Boise High R.O.T.C. and the Boy Scouts also joined the work force, and lunch was served to all of the volunteers. Morrison-Knudsen Co. offered the city free use of any of its equipment.[9] The target date for the beginning of airmail flights, announced February 26, was April 6, 1926. There wasn't much time and very little money to complete an airport in time for the great day, but community support was strong.

On February 25, 1926, Boise's city council accepted plans submitted by architect Frederick C. Hummel for a 50 x 100 foot hangar. Construction was begun on March 15, after delays caused by problems with grading the field. Even though a steam roller was used for flattening, there were still rough spots caused by the lumpy, rounded river rocks that had once been part of the stream bed.[10] In fact, an 1885 map of what was to become Boise's airfield labeled it all as a "gravel bar."

The first airmail planes to arrive in Boise, on Saturday, February 27, 1926, didn't fly in. They came by train. Chris DeVelschow, Varney's chief mechanic, picked up the first three Swallows, still in crates, at the Union Pacific freight depot on Front Street and hauled them by truck to the city garage for assembly.[11] The crew of mechanics who would put the planes together came from San Francisco, as did the Curtiss inline engines. (These would soon prove unsatisfactory, and would be replaced with more

ISHS 77-14.43

powerful Wright air-cooled radials in mid April.) Varney chief pilot Leon D. Cuddeback took one of the Swallow planes for a trial flight on March 26, 1926, and said his "big gray bird" worked like a charm. Cuddeback's responsibilities included overseeing construction of the fields and hangars at Pasco and Elko, both being built by public spirited citizens of those towns.[12]

In Boise, enthusiasm for the arrival of the city's air age ran high. City leaders began planning an "Airmail Celebration" to include a big parade and entertainment that would last far into the night. Four bands agreed to play and Boise Basque and Chinese communities signed up for the parade, as did the Y.W.C.A. and the Boise Polo Club.[13] On March 18, the celebration was billed as an "Airport Carnival," to include a "military parade, salute, dedication and jubilee." J.L. Eberle, chairman of the committee in charge, hoped to secure a "speaker of national prominence" for the occasion.[14]

On March 29, while pilot Cuddeback was running test flights on the newly assembled Swallow mail planes, a much larger visitor landed at the airport. A U.S. Army De Havilland bomber, its engines generating 400 horsepower, put down "without difficulty" on the new field. The pilot praised the facilities and called them "second to none," according to The *Statesman.*[15] In a big ad run March 31, the people of Boise valley were urged to "Greet Idaho Air Transportation" at the Boise Airport Festival on April 6, 1926. "See Idaho's first army designated airport," read the ad. "Mingle with army and airmail pilots — Weiser roundup celebrities — bewhiskered Nampans — in fact every live wire from Twin Falls to Baker will be in Boise to witness the kick-off of the Idaho spirit of progress which will soon bring an air landing field to every town in the great Snake River valley. Put on Your Ten Gallon Hat and Come!"[16]

Boise's big airmail parade included four bands and colorful floats. Many spectators wore cowboy gear: "Before noon downtown streets were lined with aviation enthusiasts, adorned with tri-colored hat bands, six-gallon hats, hoop skirts of the early '80s, corduroy trousers and

Cyril C. Thompson, left, hands a package of prize Idaho potatoes addressed to President Calvin Coolidge to Leo D. Cuddeback. Postmaster L. W. Thrailkill looks on. Boise, April 6, 1926.

Courtesy Chet Moulton

wide leather belts of cow punching days. Airplanes were droning in the air and the spirit of modern progress vied with that of the pioneer." More than 1,100 people were in a procession that took over an hour to pass through the city. Postal employees drew loud applause as mailmen pulled a miniature airplane, others sorted mail on a float, and Miss Frances Schermerhorn of the postmaster's office wore the white gown and crown of "Miss Liberty." Bessie Falk, a Boise High student was chosen "airport queen" by vote of girls at the school. She and her six attendants, dressed in white "aviatrix costumes," complete with helmets and goggles, christened one of the planes. Governor C.C. Moore gave a short speech in which he predicted that air passenger travel would someday be as common as automobile travel had become in a few short years.[17]

Automobiles lined both sides of the half-mile field as more than 2,000 people waited in holiday mood for the first sight of the plane that had taken off from Pasco at 6 o'clock that morning with Leon D. Cuddeback at the controls. George Buck and Franklin Rose had both wanted the honor of making the historic flight, and Chief Pilot Cuddeback told them to "draw straws, cut cards or roll the dice for it."[18] Cuddeback planned to fly from Elko to Boise, arriving in time for the celebration, but all of this was rescheduled in a hurry when engine trouble caused George Buck and Joe Taff to make a forced landing five miles out of Pasco. The Swallow was not seriously damaged, but Cuddeback had to fly to Pasco in a hurry with another plane to make the historic run. Franklin Rose flew to Elko to take over the flight to Boise, replacing Cuddeback.[19]

"Then, through the rising mist, at a few minutes past 10 o'clock, appeared the grey bird which left Pasco at 6 o'clock. It came low from over the Union Pacific passenger station, whirred to the south of the field, and came gliding in over Broadway, touching the yellow sands at 10:10. It turned about, taxied back to the near end, and its pilot, Leon D. Cuddeback, was welcomed by Postmaster L.W. Thrailkill, Mayor Ern G. Eagleson, and Cyril C. Thompson of the American Legion." Cuddeback was on the ground in Boise just long enough to unload some mail, refuel the plane, pick up a package of two "prize" Idaho potatoes addressed to President Calvin Coolidge, and take off again for Elko. He arrived there at 12:38 p.m., only slightly behind schedule despite time for ceremonies at Boise, and severe thunderstorms and torrential rains over the mountains.

Franklin Rose, flying the northbound mail

from Elko that inaugural day, was jinxed from the start. First, the westbound transcontinental plane was more than an hour late, delaying his takeoff until 4:00 p.m. instead of 1:20. Then he ran into the same storm Cuddeback had experienced, only far worse. His little Swallow biplane was buffeted and tossed around, throwing him completely off course. While Boise crowds celebrated and watched for his arrival, Rose was in serious trouble. He made one forced landing at Deep Creek with a sputtering engine, made his own adjustments after calling Elko for advice, then took off again. When he had not arrived by dark, search parties were hurriedly organized, but only Cuddeback had a flyable plane. *The Idaho Statesman* summarized the Varney Company's string of bad luck, primarily due to late delivery of the Swallow planes from Wichita, leaving inadequate time for thorough testing to get all the "bugs" out: "When Rose disappeared, two planes, one unassembled, were left at Boise without pilots, two pilots were at Pasco without serviceable planes, and Cuddeback was the only cog in the mechanism left in working order."[21] Art Walters, who had been giving passenger rides all day as part of the airport festival, was hired to take the Boise mail to Pasco.

Army planes were enlisted to join Leon Cuddeback in an aerial search that began at dawn April 7, 1926. Automobiles had already set out along the few roads across the bleak stretch where Rose was thought to have gone down. Not until 8:20 p.m. did news get through to Charles T. Wrightson, business manager for Varney, that Rose was safe at a remote Owyhee County ranch. He had landed without damage in a plowed field, 65 miles south of Jordan Valley, Oregon, but the plane was mired in mud due to the heavy rains. After walking to the Earl Brace ranch, he borrowed a horse and rode nearly 50 miles to the nearest telephone at the Prince Hardesty ranch.[22] His greatest concern, he said on arrival in Boise, was "to get word through here so Wrightson and the rest wouldn't have the whole United States looking for me."[23]

Boise Chamber of Commerce members gave him a hero's welcome that was more embarrassing than gratifying. He, like all of the Varney people, especially the mechanics who had worked literally night and day to get the planes ready by April 6, were understandably disappointed that so much had gone wrong.[24] They could hardly realize at the time that history would consider April 6, 1926, the start of commercial aviation in the United States, and that 50 years later a U.S. postage stamp would be issued bearing a picture of Cuddeback's Swallow biplane. They certainly could not have foreseen that in only a few years Varney would merge with other companies to form United Air Lines, for decades the world's largest, or that United would continue to celebrate April 6, 1926, as its founding date.[25]

The 90-horse Curtiss in-line engines just weren't powerful enough to get the Swallow planes over the mountains along the Varney route, and the company had to ask the Postmaster General for a 60-day grace period to replace them with 150-horsepower Wright Whirlwind air-cooled radials.[26] The Whirlwind, invented by Charles Lawrance, was a revolutionary advance in aircraft engines. Although more difficult to streamline than in-line engines, the fact that it was air-cooled eliminated the need for expensive and difficult to maintain water-cooled systems. Described by one aviation historian as "a world beater," the Wright Whirlwind was used by Charles A. Lindbergh in 1927 for his epic flight to Paris in the Ryan *Spirit of St. Louis*.[27]

Varney Swallow mail plane in flight over Idaho.

ISHS 77-14.32

ISHS 77-14.51

Courtesy Robert R. Auth

Varney mechanics with newly arrived 150 h.p. Wright Whirlwind engines. Chief pilot Cuddeback is second from right, Charles Wrightson, far right.

Pilot Joseph W. Taff.

Courtesy Robert R. Auth

Manager Charles T. Wrightson.

Service was resumed on June 1, 1926. The original Varney crew headquartered at Boise was made up of Charles T. Wrightson, Route Superintendent; Frank T. Bell, Traffic Manager; Christian DeVelschow, Chief Mechanic; Ralph Fifer and Tom Gerard, Assistant Mechanics. The pilots were Leon D. Cuddeback, Chief; Franklin Rose, George Buck and Joseph Taff. William Sanborn, a young Californian who had served in France with the flying corps during the war, joined the Boise crew later in 1926. He was killed near King Hill on April 15, 1927, while flying the mail from Salt Lake City to Boise.[28] (The airline's southern terminus had recently been transferred from Elko to the Utah capital, to make better connections with other routes). Sanborn was the first Varney pilot to lose his life, but not the last.

Flying conditions varied so much along the route between Salt Lake City, Boise and Pasco, that records could be set with the help of a tail wind, or long delays and forced landings result from headwinds or other bad weather. Planes bucking headwinds sometimes ran out of gas short of their destinations. Mail pilot Paul Scott rode tail winds to set a new record, Boise to Salt Lake, on May 17, 1927, of two and a half hours over a run scheduled for four. George Buck, battling wind and sandstorms that same week, needed four hours to get to Pasco from Boise on a trip that usually took little more than half that.[29] To make night flying safer, the federal government installed a series of navigational aids after 1927 along the routes flown by the Varney pilots; beacon lights and acetylene blinkers were placed at intervals across Idaho. Another significant advance in flying safety was enlargement of the Boise municipal airport and construction of a number of others across the state. Even for the little Swallows, with their slow 45 mile per hour landing speed, Boise's field was too short for safety. It was also plagued by poles, wires, and trees at the ends of the runways that caused frequent mishaps. One of the Army De Havilland bombers in town for the April airport festival in 1926 had narrowly escaped disaster when the pilot had to pull up at the last minute after overshooting the short runway.[30] Larger planes needed longer runways and the city fathers would hear plenty

Courtesy Robert R. Auth

Chief Pilot Leon D. Cuddeback.

about it in the late '20s and throughout the '30s. Again, it was Cyril Thompson of the American Legion who led the way in community organization to lengthen the field and remove obstructions. In June, 1927, Thompson was elected president of the Idaho Airways Association, an affiliate of the National Airways Association, and announced that his organization would "endeavor to arouse a new interest in air transportation throughout Idaho and (not be) satisfied until every town and hamlet in the state (had) a landing field adequately marked and large enough to accommodate passenger carrying ships."[31]

In a cogent article in the *Idaho Statesman* of July 24, 1927, Cyril Thompson laid out a blueprint that would be followed in the years ahead to develop Idaho's airways: "The association is interested in promoting the airmail service, commercial transportation by air, defense against insects injurious to vegetation. The immediate objective is the marking of roofs at frequent intervals for several miles on each

ISHS 77-14.34/b

ISHS 68-107

Wreckage of the Swallow mail plane that crashed near King Hill, Idaho, April 15, 1927, killing pilot William Sanborn, and wooden cross erected at the spot in his memory.

side of proposed air lines, the construction, marking and mapping of airports and emergency landing fields,and to provide a clearing house for dependable information on all questions relating to air navigation in Idaho."[32] The Idaho Airways Association's objectives would be taken over and pursued after 1929 by a new state aeronautics division in the Department of Public Works.

Idaho towns across the state became infected with airport fever in 1927, not only because of the publicity generated by the Idaho Airways Association and an equally active Spokane group, but even more by a general wave of aviation euphoria that followed Charles Lindbergh's solo flight across the Atlantic in May, 1927. Rarely, if ever, had an unknown young man become an international hero in such a short time. Idaho's Senator William E. Borah expressed, with his own special eloquence, how the country felt about Lindy: "The spirit of American youth incarnate — the spirit which charms and subdues to its purpose all things. That is what the feat of Charlie Lindbergh means to me. Nothing could be more simple, sincere and courageous. It ought to lift every American boy into the atmosphere of the heroic — life is worthwhile."[33]

The news that Lindbergh would be in Idaho on September 4, 1927, kept the interest in airport building high and after his visit, town after town took action. Burley, which already had a field, made improvements that year and nearby Rupert built a new one on a 30-acre piece of farm land. John Brockie, a local sheep rancher, already had a plane and his own pilot, Russell Owens. Brockie built a hangar at the Rupert field and Owens inaugurated the facility with stunt flying.[34] Caldwell's municipal airport site was chosen in November, 1927, on a farm field where Weber J. Appel had been giving flying lessons since 1920. He had built a hangar there in 1924, and had acquired several more planes before a student carelessly laid a burning cigarette on the wing of one of them. The highly flammable dope, with which the stretched fabric was treated to make it waterproof, burst into flame, and in a few minutes hangar, planes and all were gone. Years later Appel recalled that he and his friends and students had to maintain the Caldwell field themselves if they wanted to keep flying. This usually meant mowing sweet clover and weeds on the runways. An airport committee, appointed in December, 1927, was given a small budget, but the money was often diverted to other city projects. In 1934 the allotment was $500, but by 1937 had been cut to $200.[35]

In mid 1927 Varney Air Lines ordered Stearman biplanes with more power and mail capacity to replace the little Swallows that had

Courtesy Robert R. Auth

"Bull" Stearman biplanes like this one replaced the small Swallows. They were bigger and more powerful.

been used in the pioneering flights of 1926. On January 16, 1928, Fred Hoyt of the Stearman company was reported missing in a snowstorm between Salt Lake City and Boise while ferrying a new plane from the factory at Wichita. Planes from all over southern Idaho and Utah went out in bitter winter weather to look for the lost pilot. Leon Cuddeback, Paul Andert and C.C. Price flew Varney's search planes, and Boeing Air Transport, the U.S. Army, and private pilots joined in. Other Varney pilots on regular mail runs to and from Salt Lake also scouted the snowy mountain areas along the route. These included Harold Buckner, with Frank Rastner as observer, and Paul Scott. Russell Owen, John Brockie's private pilot, also searched the remote area.[36]

Fred Hoyt's body was found on January 12, 1928, a week after he had been forced to parachute from his ice-laden plane. A diary found with him revealed the tragic fact that he had landed safely and had lived 24 hours before dying of exposure. In it was also a poignant farewell letter to his bride of only one month.[37] Walter Varney recalled that Hoyt had once worked for him as a flight instructor, and that "after the war (he) obtained a Jennie and barnstormed the northwest, at a time when airplanes were a novelty in most western towns. He joined the Stearman company in California, and after the firm moved to Wichita, Hoyt became sales manager and a part owner."[38] Lloyd Stearman, president of the company, came west to join in the search for Hoyt, and George Hoyt, the lost flier's brother, came up from California. The two then accompanied the body to Santa Monica where the funeral was held.[39]

"Dogs are such frequent passengers on the Varney Air Mail planes that wags of the service call it "Canine's Ferry" wrote a newspaper reporter on March 2, 1928. Nearly every pilot

Courtesy Robert R. Auth

Top, left to right: Airmail pilots Clarence C. Price, Kenneth Negst, and George Buck. Above: Arthur Davidson. All flew for Varney between 1926 and 1928.

had a dog, but the veteran of them all was Joe Taff's "Ace," a German Shepherd-Timber Wolf cross, who made nearly every trip with his master. When Joe appeared in his flying suit and headed for the plane, Ace barked joyously, ran ahead and scrambled into the mail compartment.[40] No mention was made of Ace in a March 12 account of a forced landing Taff had to make at LaGrande, Oregon, because of dense fog that caused him to lose his bearings. When he found himself over Bend, Oregon, he flew to LaGrande.[41] Bad weather that month disrupted airmail flights all over the west. The Salt Lake-Pasco run was suspended for a day, and all east-west flights across the country were hours late.[42] George Buck, Varney pilot, posed for a comic picture at that time showing what a well-equipped airmail flier ought to carry with him in case of a forced landing in the wilds: a ham, a loaf of bread, a carrier pigeon, a canteen, an axe, a knife, a pistol, a shotgun, and a motor generator for emergency lighting.[43] The dangers were real, but the young pilots faced them with humor rather than grim foreboding. "They view with almost horrified disdain anyone who speaks of aviation as a particularly dangerous pursuit; they regard the difficulties of a high windstorm as all in the day's work . . .[44]

ISBN 77-14.3/a

The Air Way Inn at Boise Municipal Airport was a gathering place for Varney pilots and mechanics in the late Twenties.

Courtesy Robert R. Auth

"Doc" Eefsen and C.C. Price, Varney Airmail pilots. Eefsen became chief pilot after Cuddeback was promoted to a desk job. Price was killed at Portland when his plane hit the Interstate Bridge in fog.

ISHS 63-87.3

Lionel Kay was pilot of this Bull Stearman when an airmail publicity photo was taken with Senator William E. Borah, Governor Baldridge and Boise Mayor Hansen.

By 1928 the Varney pilots flying the mail over Idaho were Cuddeback, Buck, Taff and Rose of the original crew, and P.P. Scott, C.C. Price, Paul Andert, Harold Buckner and Lionel Kay. Four new Stearman C-Bs were put in service on the Boise to Salt Lake run, their extra size and power shortening the flight by an hour over the best the Swallows could do. Walter Varney advanced Leon Cuddeback to general manager of the airline in July and the two began investigating multi-engine planes for the passenger service they hoped to inaugurate in the spring of 1929.[45]

A Ford Trimotor landed at Boise airport on July 21, 1928, en route to Seattle where it would be used for passenger service by British Columbia Airway Corporation. The Ford would carry 14 passengers. This was "by far" the largest plane ever to land at Boise's small riverside field, but observers said it had no difficulty.[46] Another Ford Trimotor landed in Boise on November 13 en route from the Detroit factory to Spokane. A week later it crashed, killing the pilot and two passengers.[47]

A new airmail rate of five cents for the first ounce and 10 cents for each additional ounce went into effect on August 1, 1928, and greatly increased the volume of airmail out of Boise. Local people used the occasion to publicize the city's status as an airmail center by sending special greetings to friends — a promotion the Chamber of Commerce had urged.[48]

National Parks Airways, Inc., which had begun flying the mail between Salt Lake City and Great Falls, Montana, in July, flew its first passengers on August 1, 1928. On September 4 one of the company's new Universal-Fokker monoplanes crashed at Pocatello, killing the pilot and all six passengers. Mechanical failure of undetermined nature was suspected, since the plane had appeared to be laboring as it passed over Blackfoot.[49] Less than five weeks later Harry McDougall of Boise and his sister-in-law would die in a second Pocatello crash.

Courtesy Robert R. Auth

Pilot Harold C. Buckner did not survive a crash in the Blue Mountains, January, 1929. He left a wife and two children.

A Christmas rush in airmail volume led Varney to fly planes in pairs on the regular schedule in December, 1928. Pilots reported great discomfort due to cold, despite their heavy flying suits. Open cockpit flying in winter was pretty miserable, even in clear weather.[50] On January 18, 1929, Harold Buckner was reported missing somewhere between Boise and Pasco. Next day he was reported safe in an isolated trapper's cabin near Cove, Oregon, but with broken arms, legs and ribs received in his crash in the remote mountain area. One of the trappers who found him had walked eight miles through six feet of snow to the nearest forest service telephone. On January 19, Charles Wrightson left La Grande with a doctor and box sled to bring Buckner back to the hospital, but before they arrived the pilot was dead of injuries so serious the doctor said no emergency measures could have saved him, even if help had arrived sooner. Buckner left a wife and two children in Boise. Like most airmail pilots, he had learned to fly during the war and had later been an instructor while retaining a reserve commission. He was given a military funeral in San Francisco.[51] More than 30 years later an antique plane buff recovered parts of Buckner's Stearman C-B from the Wallowa Mountain site and built them into the plane he was then restoring.[52]

Paul Andert narrowly missed a forced landing in the Great Salt Lake on February 3, 1929, which would surely have been fatal. His engine froze up over Kelton, Utah, just five minutes before he reached the lake, giving him time to make a landing.[53] The same storm caused a National Parks Airways plane to come down near Malad, Idaho, on its way from Pocatello to Salt Lake City.[54]

Abe Warner, veteran Varney mail pilot stationed at Boise, landed his burning plane at Baker, Oregon, on August 22, 1930, with a leaking fuel line spraying gasoline into the cockpit. Despite serious burns, he calmly pulled the mail sacks out of the forward compartment just before the gasoline tanks exploded. The fabric on one wing was nearly burned off before Warner got the ship to the ground; the explosion destroyed all but the engine. On February 14, 1931, the President was authorized to award a Congressional Medal of Honor to any person employed as a pilot in the Air Mail Service of the United States who distinguished himself by heroism or extraordinary achievement while carrying the mail.[56] Abe Warner was the second man to receive the medal, awarded in December, 1932. *Collier's* magazine published the story of the exploit that earned the medal for Warner in its January 7, 1933, issue. Abe Warner's real name was Roy H. Warner, but he had been tagged with the nickname "Honest Abe" after an episode early in his flying career when he accidentally carried another man's tool kit home with him after work. He turned his car around and drove six miles back to the field to return it.[57]

Other Varney mail pilots had nicknames too. Clarence C. Price was called "Cash and Carry" because he usually went by the initials C.C. He was killed at Portland when he hit the Interstate bridge while landing. Walter E. Eefsen, chief pilot for Varney after Cuddeback's pro-

Courtesy Wayne White

Courtesy Robert R. Auth

Christian DeVelschow was Varney's chief mechanic in the early years at Boise.

Courtesy Robert R. Auth

Top: Little Bobby Krall stands next to the wreck of a Boeing 40B near Boise. His mother Florence ran the Air Way Inn. Note passenger compartment window at right. Above: Ivan Nelson was the first manager of Boise Municipal Airport, 1926-1931.

motion, was given the nickname "Doc" by Barney Barnard, a mechanic at Salt Lake City after he dropped some medical supplies to an ill and isolated radio operator.[58]

The earliest fliers to test their wings over Idaho couldn't get insurance at all. Mail pilots of the 1930s could, but they paid the highest premiums of any professionals in the state. "Cloud dodging with the United States mail is a job which receives a heroic halo and a romantic flutter from the movies and fiction writers." noted an *Idaho Statesman* reporter, "but the fun drops out when they get their insurance premium bills . . . the occupation is rated at the top of the list for danger and high prices." Race horse jockeying was listed second most dangerous.[59] That some of Idaho's pioneer mail pilots lived to a ripe old age, like Leon D. Cuddeback, who made that first historic flight on April 6, 1926, was due to a combination of skill, good judgment, luck, and early retirement from active flying. For far too many, bad luck alone was enough to send them to early graves, no matter how skillful or brave they were. The odds, confirmed by actuarial tables, were against them.

MOUNTAIN PILOTS VI

The first extensive flying over Idaho's mountains was done by U.S. Army pilots "for the protection of the forest areas of the United States against destruction by fire," in the language of the May, 1920, bill authorizing the funding. The Secretary of Agriculture was to request aerial patrols from the Secretary of War as needed.[1]

In February, 1925, Congress appropriated $50,000 to the Agriculture department for aerial patrol of national forests in the Pacific Northwest. Idaho was to be covered by planes out of Boise, Missoula, and Spokane.[2] These cities, along with Cascade later on, have continued to be the headquarters for mountain fliers to the present day.

In April, 1925, the Independence Placer Mining Company arranged with a Spokane commercial flier to supply its remote Clearwater claims by plane. The pilot said he could haul two 12-foot sections of 20-inch steel pipe, weighing 650 pounds, on each trip, and that in 35 days could transport the entire 58 tons needed by the new camp. From the takeoff point at Iron Mountain, Montana, the plane could make a round trip every hour. The alternative available to the mining company was a pack train of mules that would take five days to cover a long and difficult trail over the Bitterroot Mountains. Company president William Fahle of Wallace had a landing area cleared of dead snags from an early-day forest fire near the 1860s mining camp of Moose City. "A landing field, so-called, (was) prepared. 'Twas not so deep as a well, nor so wide as a church, but 'twas enough." The plane made several trips in the summer of 1925 before knocking off a wing on takeoff. Deep snows of winter grounded the plane for the season before repairs had been completed.

Fahle explained the economics that had led him to pioneer aerial supply to his mine. "A plane could make six or eight trips a day carrying 650 to 700 pounds each trip, while a pack animal's load was 200 pounds." The airplane was clearly cheaper and got the job done faster.[3]

Old barnstormer Nick Mamer of Spokane told Boise's Rotary Club on August 20, 1925, that the city urgently needed a good airport if it wanted to be considered for future use by Army and other fliers. He said Spokane had secured a squadron of military airplanes for forest fire patrol, primarily because the city already had built a municipal airport. Mamer, an army reservist, was flying the forest patrol at the time, and had been ferrying State Forester Ben Bush on a survey of Idaho.[4] In September, C. A. Barton, then vice president and general manager of Boise-Payette Lumber Company, and a member of the state forestry board, also took an extended flight over Idaho's mountains with Lt. R. F. Freng. He was concerned not only with the feasibility of fire patrols from the air, but with scouting out remote stands of timber to see how roads could be built to them for logging.[5]

Pilot Freng flew members of the State Land Board and Governor C. C. Moore on other excursions over most of central Idaho while he was in town, giving them an opportunity to see state and federal forests, as well as spectacular mountain scenery.[6]

Airmail pilots, who had skirted Idaho's mountains for years, and flown regularly over Oregon's Blue Mountains, were strong advocates of aviation as a way to supply back country mines. There were many natural meadows ready for safe landings right now, they said, and others that could be made ready by removing downed timber. One pilot, in response to a reporter's skepticism, had a bit of fun with him.

He asked:

"Are there any lakes up there?"

"There are," he was assured. "From one peak 30 are visible."

"It's simple then," responded the pilot with a grin. "If you get in trouble and have to come down, you can run your plane into one of those lakes. It will float long enough for you to paddle to shore, and there you are. Nobody is hurt and all you have to do is fly out again."

"But what would you do if there weren't any lakes or natural meadows within reach?" persisted the official pessimist of the crowd. "Wouldn't it be dangerous then?"

"Oh no," responded the birdman. "All you do is pick out a nice steep mountain slope, free of trees and reasonably level, and point your nose uphill. Any pilot with any degree of landing skill can land so gently on a mountainside that his passengers will think they are still flying. And then the tail of your machine acts as a brake and keeps you from rolling down hill."

Still the pessimist was not satisfied. "That's all well and good," he growled, "but suppose your hillside is heavily timbered. What do you do then?"

"Easier and easier; ask me something hard," commanded the aviator.

"You pick out for yourself a nice big, substantial tree, fairly clear of obstructions. Then you fly at it and gently hit it with one wing, all your power of course shut off. It's hard on the wing, but the rest of the plane and the passengers don't realize anything is wrong. Your plane simply whirls around that tree, sinking lower in a great spiral, until it rests on the ground."[7]

Idaho sheep rancher John "Jock" Brockie pioneered the use of an airplane to keep track of his flocks in remote areas. He bought a plane in May, 1927, and hired Russell Owen as pilot. Owen and Brockie flew regularly from Rupert over much of south central Idaho. After searching for days on horseback for a missing band and its herder in June, 1927, Brockie and Owen took to the air and found them within 20 minutes.[8] It was Brockie, as noted earlier, who built a hangar at Rupert for his plane when it was the only one in the area. Owen moved to Boise in 1928 to give flying lessons, but other pilots continued to fly for ranchers when their flocks were lost or trapped by winter snows, as happened in December, 1928, near Strevell, south of Burley. One band of 1700 sheep was caught en route from Soda Springs to Malta when 18 inches of snow fell at Meadow Brook pass. Only by dragging juniper trees behind horses was a trail broken that allowed the sheep to get through to Malta where their winter hay was stored.[9]

A Twin Falls power company used a plane to locate a break in its line to the Jarbidge, Nevada, mines that winter. Workmen were sent out from Jarbidge to make the repairs. Without aerial reconnaissance, the mining camp would have been shut down most of the winter while company men battled deep snows looking for the break along 100 miles of transmission line.[10]

Nick Mamer's Spokane flying service began carrying hunters into Idaho's isolated back country in October, 1928. His pilot, Clarence Paulsen, made a preliminary survey of the 250 mile trip from Spokane to Chamberlain Basin, with one stop at Grangeville, and a week later flew two hunters to the Stonebraker ranch.[11] (George Stonebraker was himself a mountain pilot who carried the mail to the Salmon River country in the early thirties).

Jack Rose of the Mamer service had a more unusual assignment that month. He and Idaho County Sheriff Hervey Rothwell took off from Grangeville to hunt down a mad trapper named Walter McCoy who had been terrorizing settlers in Chamberlain Basin by peeking in windows, stealing, and threatening to kill them. Once he had spotted the "wild man" from the air, the sheriff and his deputy set out from Stonebraker Ranch on horseback through deep snow, and brought him back a few days later. A Grangeville judge committed him to the asylum at Blackfoot.[12]

Fred W. Bradley of San Francisco began clearing a landing strip at his Meadow Creek gold mines in October, 1928. A tractor was pulling stumps and it was expected that the field, half a mile long and 800 feet wide, would be ready for use in the winter by planes equipped with skis.[13] George Stonebraker, who had airmail contracts, bought a new plane in January, 1931, after his five-passenger Bellanca crashed

Courtesy Dan Stohr

Penn Stohr and his ski-equipped Travelair 6000, Cascade, Idaho, 1943.

into West Mountain near Cascade while hunting cattle. Pilot Ray Fisher was killed, but his four passengers escaped with only minor injuries. Fisher had been a barnstormer with Wild Irish Bill Haddock's flying circus before going to work for Stonebraker. "Flying is as safe over the mountains around Cascade as over any other mountains," said Stonebraker after the wreck, "and a forced landing on any hilltop in trees is sure to mean a crack-up. But this doesn't mean that one accident should mar the future of a promising commercial aviation field."[14] The *Idaho Statesman* said on January 17, 1931, "Stonebraker pioneered the central Idaho region from an aviation standpoint and has established a service by air to landing fields in all communities."

A. C. Blomgren, state airway engineer, who assumed that position in 1929 when the Aeronautics Division of the Department of Public Works was established, described mountain flying in Idaho as it was at the beginning of 1931: "Mining operations, irrigation storage water development, and other activities heretofore closed down during the winter months, are enabled to continue operations throughout the year by the advent of this new mode of transportation.

"As an example the construction camp of 60 men at Deadwood Basin was supplied with necessities of life during the winter of 1929 and 1930. Daily trips by a plane equipped with skis were made from Boise and Cascade, carrying in men, mail and supplies and bringing out the sick or hurt to receive competent medical attention. Several lives were saved in this manner.

"Daily trips, weather permitting, are made carrying passengers, mail and supplies from Cascade to Knox, Yellow Pine, Meadow Creek and Deadwood Basin. Briefly, the route flown is from Cascade, the operating base, to Knox, an airline distance of 22 miles, thence to the field on Johnson Creek, just below Yellow Pine, thence to Meadow Creek. Retracing the route to Knox and thence to Deadwood Basin, a distance of 22 miles, and another 22 miles to

Courtesy Robert L. Hagar

This Zenith Z6 cabin plane, photographed at McCall in 1934, was flown from an open cockpit -- an arrangement like that of the Boeing 40B. Left to right: Mrs. Albert Hagar, Bobby Hagar and Lily May Hagar.

Cascade." Blomgren pointed out the obvious advantage of flying the mail and supplies as compared to using dogsleds in winter as had been done historically. With 60 men working near Yellow Pine, regular mail was important.[15] Wild Bill Haddock provided his aerial service in the winter of 1930-31, using a ski-equipped six passenger Travelair. Paul McKinley and William Gowen were Haddock's pilots.[16]

Mountain rescues of stranded and injured people were a regular challenge for mountain pilots. In March, 1931, William Gowen flew the Haddock Travelair to an improvised landing area in a small pasture at the old Caswell ranch near Big Creek to pick up Noel Routson, a young forest service employee, who had been struck by an avalanche of snow and rocks while working on a forest trail. Gowen landed on the postage-stamp field, loaded his passenger into the flying ambulance, and after a brief stop at Cascade carried him on to Boise where he was taken to a hospital. Although his crew mates had feared that Routson's injuries might prove fatal, they were found to be minor.[17]

A.A. Bennett, operating a flying service out of Boise, made two ambulance rescues within a week in 1931. On October 31, he made the first flight ever into a new airstrip at Atlanta to bring out Everett Farnham, forest ranger, who had accidentally shot himself in the leg while dismounting from a horse. Bennett made, in a 59 minute round trip, what would have taken more than four hours one way by road. On November 9 Bennett flew to Yellow Pine to pick up Don Keller who had suffered a broken leg in a cave-in at the Meadow Creek mine. Both mountain landings were in light snow without skis.[18] Another Atlanta worker was brought out by Bob King, flying for Bennett, on November 12, after a log rolled on him causing serious back injuries. King's plane reached Atlanta only an hour after the accident. It was King who usually flew the mail to the old mining camp that winter after Bennett Air Transport got the contract.[19]

William Gowen and two passengers escaped injury when his plane crash landed at Warrens on December 24, 1931, during an attempted takeoff with skis. The field was so sticky he couldn't pick up enough speed to clear the runway. All he could do was cut power and drop back to earth before he was too high. The Travelair was badly damaged, and the passengers who were flying out for Christmas never made it, but were thankful to be alive, even though they spent the holiday in Warrens.[20]

Similar conditions prevented a plane from taking off from Atlanta in January, 1932. A forest ranger who had lost three fingers in an accident with a circular saw, had to wait several days before conditions allowed either takeoff or landing from the snowbound field. Snow and fog delayed airmail flights all over Idaho that winter, and other commercial fliers were grounded. Bennett Air Transport succeeded in delivering the mail to Knox, Warren, Yellow Pine and Deadwood, but only by "bombing" those places with mail sacks. Men on skis or snowshoes went out to pick them up. Atlanta's mail was delayed so long that over 300 pounds of it had accumulated before a plane got through. By that time people in the isolated town were longing for oranges, lettuce, and other fresh produce. Two crates of eggs were delivered in March without cracking a one.[21]

In April Bob Johnson of Missoula came to Boise to fly A.A. Bennett's mail run to Atlanta. One of Bennett's planes was under repair, and this enabled him to fulfill his contract.[22] The partnership was expected to last only a month or two, but lasted three years. Bennett had flown with Johnson at Missoula before forming his own company in Boise, and as Johnson remembered it years later, Bennett asked him to join him in the winter of 1931-32 because "he had more flying than he could handle." He also remembered that working with Bennett was not easy. "I couldn't stay ahead of Bennett. I paid bills and paid bills that he'd run up and I finally had to quit. He wouldn't pay a bill until he had to . . . I couldn't stick down there in Boise and pay his bills any longer . . .[23]

When new contracts were let on the mail routes Bennett had been covering, Johnson Flying Service of Missoula was the low bidder. For the next eight years Bob Johnson and his pilots flew the back country from Cascade, McCall, Missoula and Boise, not only delivering the mail, but hauling freight and passengers as well. Johnson's favorite plane, the workhorse of those years, was a Travelair powered by a Wright Whirlwind radial engine. The ship, named the *Mae Gerard,* was lost at Deadwood Lake when it sank through the ice and had to be hauled ashore. As Johnson and Art Pritzl worked with a small heater to melt ice on the control cables, gas fumes ignited, causing an explosion and fire that destroyed the plane in minutes.[24]

During the years Johnson flew the "snowline run" he often had to battle competition from other fliers. As he recalled later, "They tried to run me out of business. I didn't run worth a damn. I flew weather they didn't dare touch . . . I knew my country and I flew those snowstorms; I was doing it all the time and they weren't . . . when they'd be sitting on the ground, I'd come in and unload and load and go out . . . I suppose they thought, 'This crazy bastard, he's going to get killed . . .' You learned something on those flights and you better remember it . . ." Bob Johnson's recollections of Boise were not happy ones, not only because of his experiences with Bennett, but because a number of Boise flying services undercut him drastically in an attempt to get his back country commercial business.[25] The reputation Johnson Flying Service established over the years, with great pilots like Penn Stohr, kept them in business when others failed.

The winter of 1931-32, highlighted by flights

ISHS 76-216.1

Lamoine Stevens of Twin Falls was one of the first to stock Idaho lakes with fish from an airplane. Photo circa 1930.

Courtesy Dan Stohr

Johnson Flying Service, with headquarters in Missoula, had Idaho bases in Boise (above), Cascade, and McCall.

like those above, may be regarded as the real beginning of back country flying in Idaho. That was the season in which the flying service was reliable enough that mining companies began to regard it as essential to year-round operation for them. It has continued to be the lifeline to isolated mountain towns ever since. 1931-32 was also the year that mountain pilots began to be viewed by feature writers and the public as modern-day heroes whose every exploit was worth reporting. The winter of 1931-32, in the words of one writer, "developed in Idaho new and modern pioneers . . . hardy, fearless and determined, who face . . . terrible dangers. These new pioneers have crossed uncharted wilderness, treacherous peaks and ravines, great snowbanks and dense fogs, all to carry food, sustenance and news of the outside world to a number of isolated and snowbound mountain mining villages."[26] The back country pilot had become a figure of romance, and many a tale would be told in the years ahead of a select few who became legendary. Bob Johnson was the subject of a book, from which some of the quotations used here are taken — Steve Smith's *Fly the Biggest Piece Back*. Others, like Ray Arnold, who still flies out of Cascade, have had their stories told in national magazines.[27]

Penn Stohr, flying for Bob Johnson out of McCall and Cascade, probably received more press than any other mountain pilot of the 1940s. Frank Wiley, in *Montana and the Sky,* says Stohr was second only to Bob Johnson as a mountain pilot, knew the rugged country of Montana and Idaho as few people will ever have the opportunity to know it, and could "get in and out of a shorter field, with a bigger load, on a hotter day, at higher elevation, than just about anyone in the business."[28]

Stohr achieved national fame in February, 1943, when he rescued five crew members of an Army B-23 bomber that had gone down on the edge of Loon Lake in a rugged mountain area north of McCall. Stohr spotted the wreck and some of the crew members while on his regular run from Cascade to Warren. "I noticed the tops of a string of trees had been clipped off on the south shore of Loon Lake," he told a reporter on the evening of February 13, 1943. "When I got over the lake, I saw the army bomber. It was a two motored plane, and it was lying on its belly at a 45-degree angle to the lake, and about 50 feet from the shore. The wings appeared to have been sheared off as the plane landed. The fuselage did not appear to be damaged. I saw three men while I was over the spot. They had a flagpole stuck up on a log stage they had built on the ice of the lake, with one of the men's shirts flapping in the breeze."

Five of the eight-man crew were still with the plane and three others had started to walk out for help. The plane had been down 15 days

Courtesy Dan Stohr

Mountain pilot Penn Stohr was seldom seen without his cigar.

before Penn Stohr spotted it on February 13. On the 14th he set his ski-equipped Travelair down on the frozen lake and flew the men out to Cascade. Only Sgt. Forrest Hoover was hurt. He had a broken knee cap and an arm injury. He told the sheriff upon arrival, "We managed all right, but we did get pretty hungry. We ate some chocolate bars and then we managed to kill a few squirrels. We rigged a shelter out of some old tents, and it wasn't too bad. We weren't exactly comfortable, though."[30]

The three crew members who walked out suffered from frostbite and exhaustion, but were not seriously harmed. They had been able to reach a cabin where they found the makings of pancakes, and later a CCC camp with other food. They followed a telephone line to a ranger station with a good supply of groceries. They again made pancakes, ate, and then got around to trying the telephone. It worked. A call soon brought a rescue party from McCall. After a few days rest in a Boise hospital, all were released.[31]

Penn Stohr's exploit brought him letters from all over the country, including one from the mother of one of the bomber crew, expressing her gratitude and the belief that her prayers had been heard and that God had led Stohr to the downed plane to rescue her son. Former fliers who had worked with Stohr before the war sent him clippings from newspapers across America. One young man wrote, "The rescue of those boys must have been quite an experience for you, but I guess you have done that sort of thing so much that it is just in a day's work for you anymore. I know from experience that you have made many mercy flights in your job up there and that the 'back country' depends on 'old Penn' in case of emergency."[32]

That Penn Stohr was more than just a remarkable pilot is reflected in the tributes to his memory that poured in after he was killed on June 20, 1957, near Townsend, Montana. His Ford Trimotor crashed shortly after takeoff due to mechanical failure. "Universally admired," "respected," and "loved" were words often used by those who knew him personally or by reputation. John Corlett, veteran Boise reporter, interviewed Stohr while on a flight to Stibnite with him late in 1943. "He's the idol of Long Valley and the pack horse and ofttimes saviour of the primitive area," he wrote. "Today he is indispensable — the one man who can fly the primitive area in a blinding snowstorm and come out alive." On more than one occasion when a sudden storm came up Stohr landed in the first meadow he came to, and bedded down under the wing of his plane until it blew over. He was sometimes snowed in for as long as three days, but was always able to fly out.[33]

Mountain pilots had their own tried and true ways of starting motors in sub-zero weather. Bob Johnson and Penn Stohr both heated their engines with a Coleman gasoline stove under a canvas hood. They warmed the motor oil in a five gallon can over the office stove, then poured it into the engine just before they were

Courtesy Dan Stohr

Penn Stohr and crew at Cascade with the old faithful Travelair 6000 – a favorite of mountain pilots.

Bradley Mining Company flew Travelairs in and out of Stibnite from Bradley Field in Boise.

Courtesy Doris Willy Crowder

Courtesy Harold Dougal

Ford Trimotors were flown into most Idaho back country air strips for more than 20 years. Glenn Higby was co-pilot of this one shown at Indian Creek.

Courtesy Randy Woods

Bill Woods, in coveralls, with friends at his Floating Feather airport west of Boise. The plane is a Stinson 6000 Trimotor. Woods, who called himself Old Man of the Mountains, always flew with two wire hair terriers.

Courtesy Randy Woods

Bill Woods made this forced landing on the ice beside Salmon River. It was a tough walk out.

Courtesy Randy Woods

Planes downed in the back country often had to be salvaged piece by piece. Bill Woods brought one down the Middle Fork to the nearest airstrip and put it back together.

ready to go. Once in the air there were strict rules to follow if you wanted to survive. You had to know where you were, where you were going, and where you could land if the weather suddenly turned bad. "I know every creek and canyon in Idaho and Montana and parts of Oregon and Washington," Stohr told John Corlett. "I have to because when the weather comes down I have to get into those canyons and find my way to the nearest landing field."[34]

The nearest "landing field" might be only a mountain meadow with fewer rocks and trees than the forest around it, or it might be a sand or gravel bar beside the Salmon River. In an emergency anything you could walk away from was a good landing — certainly better than being seriously injured a long way from anywhere, when nobody knew where to look for you, even if the weather let them. Back country pilots made lots of unscheduled landings, some without damage to the planes or themselves, some serious. Since crack-ups were relatively common, pilots were told to "stick with the ship" and save as much of it as they could. Parachutes were of no use anyway at the low altitudes mountain fliers flew. If they could land the plane at all, some or more of it might be salvaged.[35] It was fairly common to bring a downed plane out in pieces, either by plane, if a landing could be made nearby, or down the main Salmon or Middle Fork by raft to the nearest airstrip if that was the only alternative.

Bill Woods, who styled himself "The Old Man of the Mountains" brought one out that way in the spring of 1955. He had made a skillful forced landing on ice beside the Middle Fork, and spent four days walking in deep snow with the two wire-haired terriers who always flew with him. He was headed for the nearest help when met by Jim Larkin who was looking for him on snowshoes.[36] According to one old pilot, "Bill Woods left wrecked planes scattered all over Idaho." Maybe so, but he walked away from all of them in a career of 30 years and 29,000 hours of mountain flying. He flew horses, cows, hogs, mules, tractors, and complete lodges and the machinery to run them.[37]

Jim Larkin, who did most of his flying for the U.S. Forest Service, was honored in 1991 for flying 50 years without an accident or a violation of any kind. Jim flew more than three million miles in that time, most of them over Idaho's mountains. Glenn Higby, chief pilot for Idaho Power Company, earned his 25 year award in 1967, and also made three million miles before retiring. He is widely respected as one of the best.[38] Of the hundreds who have flown regularly over the back country, only a few can be mentioned in a general survey, but old-timers, in many hours of interviews, invariably mentioned the same names. These are their choices for a list of memorable mountain pilots: Ray Arnold, A.A. Bennett, Harold Dougal, Warren Ellison, Glen Eichelberger, Bob Fogg, Glenn Higby, Marv Hornback, Bob Johnson, Jim Larkin, Penn Stohr, George Stonebraker, Bill Woods, and Bert Zimmerly. Some of them became household names in Idaho because of particular episodes in their careers. Others remained unknown except to the fraternity of back country pilots who admired and respected them most.

Deadwood was regularly supplied in winter by Johnson Flying Service using planes on skis. Note the wind sock on a pole and pair of skis stuck in the snow.

ISHS 3671

Courtesy Boise City Archives

This fine aerial view of Boise Municipal Airport shows Table Rock, top right, the Idaho Penitentiary just below it, and the Varney Air Lines hangar next to the Broadway bridge. Photo by H.W. Stewart, 1935.

Courtesy Chet Moulton

Broadway Avenue and a close-up aerial view of the big steel hangar that was later moved to the new airport on the bench, where it still forms the core of the present terminal.

PIONEER PASSENGER CARRIERS VII

1929 was a year of intense interest in Idaho's chances of getting regularly scheduled air passenger service for the first time. Both Varney Air Lines, which had been flying the mail since April, 1926, and Mamer Flying Service of Spokane announced plans to be carrying passengers by mid-summer.[1] The key questions for both companies were: Was there enough public demand for the service to support it? Were there enough first class and emergency air fields along proposed routes for safety, and what kind of planes were best suited to the number of passengers that could be anticipated and to the flying conditions over Idaho?

The airport problems of the state were addressed early in 1929 when the Idaho legislature created a new division of aeronautics in the Department of Public Works "for the purpose of establishing a state policy of constructive cooperation in aviation development." This was to include "establishment of air navigation facilities and designation of routes; negotiations with other states in regard to interstate airways, and the issuance of maps and bulletins pertaining to airways."[2] Of greater immediate importance for air passenger service that year was an act authorizing cities, towns and counties to acquire lands for airports and to issue bonds and levy taxes for their construction and maintenance.[3]

Payette was the first town to ask formal approval from the state Department of Public Works for its proposed airport, just weeks after the law went into effect. The requirements were modest: "to determine that the approaches are free from obstructions and that the runways are of suitable length." Payette's Kiwanis club was the sponsor of this project.[4]

Boise's riverside airport urgently needed improvement. Almost every visiting pilot, civilian or military, had complained from the time the field was built in early 1926 that runways were too short and rough, and that tall trees and wires at the ends of the field were dangerous. Lindbergh had mentioned it in 1927, and Captain R.G. Breene, pilot for Edward E. Spafford, National President of the American Legion, was bluntly outspoken about it when the two visited the city in April, 1928. "A most dangerous field" was his appraisal. "Boise can never expect to be a terminal with such a field. Cut the wires down on the east and increase the length by not less than 500 feet.

"I'll never come back," he said, "at least by airplane, until I hear of real improvements made on the field. I'll be damned glad when I get off . . ." When the plane stalled on its first attempt to take off, Breene taxied around and shouted at reporters, "I told you so." Commander Spafford added, "No one will come into this field on my recommendation." It took three tries before Spafford's plane "slithered" across the sand and finally became airborne. City officials no doubt squirmed in embarrassment, for a large contingent was on hand to see the Legion commander on his way.[5]

On June 6, 1929, Boise voters approved a $78,000 bond issue for airport improvement 2393 to 536. The city's two newspapers had taken opposite sides on the question, the *Boise Capital News* strongly supportive and the *Idaho Daily Statesman* negative, or at best skeptical. "Instead of thinking of the future of the aviation interests constantly," editorialized the *Statesman,* "Why not think about the future of the taxpayer for awhile?"[6] Boise taxpayers evidently agreed, and defeated an

ISHS 70-190.42

The Varney drive-through hangar shortly after United Air Lines was formed. The small letters under "United" read "Varney Air Lines Division," a name soon dropped.

$85,000 bond issue in April, but overwhelmingly approved $78,000 a month later. At issue in the two campaigns was whether or not Boiseans were "air-minded." Antis defensively insisted they were, but voted against the bonding anyway.[7]

Both Varney and Mamer considered trimotor planes for their proposed passenger lines. Nick Mamer, pioneer barnstormer and back country commercial flier, flew to Boise several times in the spring of 1929 in a Ford Trimotor, one of a fleet of three his company planned to use in an ambitious 16 city network that would include Seattle, Portland, Spokane, Boise and Butte. Mamer tested public interest in the new service by giving Boiseans a chance to ride in the 14 passenger Ford. The *Capital News* called it "the mightiest mechanical bird of the air," and said "No ship that has reached this port has attracted greater attention." A reporter who rode the plane from Emmett to Boise was ecstatic over the experience, describing it as "a floating Pullman with a passenger-carrying capacity of 14, two pilots and mechanics, all perfectly housed, away from the noise of

Courtesy Chet Moulton

A closer view of the Varney hangar, shortly after its completion in 1931. Boise State University's Bronco Stadium now occupies most of the area shown south of the river.

the 300-horsepower motors, the annoyance of wind and cold."[8] The trimotor gave rides to 310 people on a day when 2,000 people turned out to see the big ship.[9]

Mamer also struck a deal with Boise Flying Service to add a Boise to Pocatello passenger and freight connection using its four passenger Ryan Brougham, a plane very similar to Lindbergh's *Spirit of St. Louis.* Both companies said service would begin July 1, 1929, but Mamer told Boise its field needed re-surfacing immediately for successful passenger operations.[10]

Carrying out his responsibilities under the new laws, first state aeronautics director Arthur C. Blomgren worked with Nick Mamer and George Carter Miller, federal aeronautics adviser, to map out a route between Boise and Spokane that would have adequate marking, navigational aids, and emergency landing fields. None of the towns between the two terminal cities was yet ready for Ford Trimotors, but several had plans, or were already starting to build new fields.[11] A.A. Goodman of McCall, for example, was grubbing out a field all by himself and trying to interest others in the project. As secretary of the McCall Chamber of Commerce he could see the potential for making his town on the shores of Payette Lake a destination for vacationing fliers.[12]

Arthur Blomgren and U.S. Department of Commerce officials visited many Idaho towns in May, 1929, inspecting sites for proposed local airports or improvements to existing ones. They went to Hailey, Twin Falls, Gooding, Challis, Payette and Pocatello. Later that year they visited Blackfoot, Idaho Falls, Rigby, Rexburg, St. Anthony, Ashton, Nampa, Caldwell, Jerome, Grangeville, Wallace, Rupert, Sandpoint and McCall. Idaho truly had airport fever, and the state was actively planning for the new aviation age.[13]

A Western States Airways Conference was held in Boise July 8-10, 1929, hosted and organized by Governor H.C. Baldridge. The governors of Utah, Nevada, Wyoming and Oregon came, and each chaired a special session of the three day meet. Philip G. Johnson, president of Boeing Air Transport, the superintendent of Yellowstone National Park,

Courtesy Robert R. Auth

Ellen Church, United Air Lines' first stewardess, is shown here beside a Boeing 247 with a logo that still carries the Varney name.

Courtesy Boise City Archives

National Airmail Week, 1938, was celebrated in style. Pilots from all over Idaho flew the mail to Boise to be put on this Boeing 247. Those present include Penn Stohr, second from left, and Frances Schermerhorn of the Post Office, center, next to the stewardess. The plane fits easily inside the Varney hangar.

and numerous federal officials from War, Navy, Commerce and Post Office departments took part. The Western Association of State Highway Officials decided to hold its own meeting in Boise concurrently to share mutual transportation concerns. The State of Idaho was widely praised for taking the leadership role in planning for the future of commercial aviation in the West.[14]

When Varney Air Lines began flying passengers in May, 1930, it was not with Ford Trimotors but with Boeing 40-B4s — biplanes with a four-passenger enclosed cabin up front and an open cockpit behind for the pilot. Boeing Air Transport had first used the Boeing 40 in July, 1927, on its San Francisco to Chicago run. The company's fleet of 25 of these rugged and dependable planes made money from the start and established Boeing's reputation as a builder of first class passenger planes.[15] The Boeing 40-C was another four-passenger version; National Parks Airways bought one for its southeast Idaho service. The line carried contract mail in the late '20s and flew its first passengers in an open-cockpit J5 Stearman with a 225 horsepower Wright engine. Later the company used an eight-passenger Fokker Universal. By 1935 the 10-passenger Boeing 247D was standard on National Parks flights between Montana and Utah.[16]

Varney Air Lines became a division of United Air Lines on July 1, 1931, through a complicated series of mergers and holding companies. The Varney name continued to be used in the logo of United planes until the division was finally absorbed totally by United Air Lines, Inc., on July 20, 1934.[17] Meanwhile, Idaho began receiving regular air service by what has been acknowledged to be the first fully modern passenger liner — the all-metal, low-wing, twin-engine, 10-passenger Boeing 247D. The new planes could carry 400 pounds of mail and express in addition to passengers, and greatly reduced the time on all scheduled runs. The 23-3/4 hours it took to fly from Boise to New York seemed like a miraculous accomplishment in 1933. The Boeing 247 had a top speed of 200 miles per hour, a cruising speed of 189 miles per hour, and a range of 745 miles. It had a thermostatically controlled heating-cooling system, dome lights, and individual reading lights. There was even a toilet — an innovation necessitated by the ship's greater cruising range.[18] Before the 247, planes stopped 14 times in crossing the country. After 1933, only seven stops were needed.[19] (Today even two seem too many!)

Pioneer Varney mail pilot Leon D. Cuddeback, who inaugurated commercial aviation in America with his historic flight of April 6, 1926, Pasco to Boise to Elko, was now vice-president of United's Seattle-Portland-Salt Lake City division. He announced on April 27, 1933, that regular service with Boeing 247s would begin in May.[20] Until enough of the new planes became available Boeing 40Bs would be used for some flights. United ordered 60 247s, and sent one of the first through Boise on April 25, 1933, on its way to Chicago where it went on display at the World's Fair. The theme of the exposition was "World of Tomorrow" and the big Boeing was not only the latest thing, but a forerunner of what passenger planes would be in the future.[21]

When those first Boeing 247Ds landed in Boise in 1933, they had the benefit of a superb steel hangar that Varney Air Lines had built in 1931. It was large enough to handle any ships in operation at the time, and featured a drive-through plan that allowed planes to taxi in under cover for servicing, then taxi out the other side for takeoff.[22]

The revolutionary Boeings were soon followed by the plane that became the world standard for passenger carrying for a generation: the Douglas DC3. Also a low-wing, twin-engine, all-metal monoplane, the DC3 was bigger and faster than 247D and made it obsolete in a hurry. United ordered 10 DC3s for one million dollars late in 1935, and began regular Mainliner service in 1936.[23] The first Mainliner did not land in Idaho, since Boise's riverside airport was declared too small for the larger planes to negotiate safely. This led directly to the city's decision, urged on by the Chamber of Commerce, to acquire land and build a much larger field on a level sagebrush bench three miles south of town.[24] Even so, as badly as Boise wanted Mainliner service, the first DC3 did not land at the new Boise Air

Courtesy Doris Willy Crowder

Courtesy Boise City Archives

Idaho pilots who flew mail to Boise for National Airmail Week, May 15-22, 1938. Top row: Earl Popp, Verne Oliver, O.A. Kelker, Lionel Dean, Lamoine Stevens, Thomas Schwarz, Boyd Swanson, Casey Jones. Bottom: Malcolm Parsons, W.H. Anderson, Van Jones, Elden Carter, Ray Crowder, Ed M. Bryan, Bob Johnson, Penn Stohr.

Left: Postal employees with mail.

Terminal until January 21, 1939.

The new field on Whitney Bench was remarkable for its size. The city bought 560 acres and leased an additional 400 acres from the state, permitting construction of an 8,800 foot runway—longest in the nation. With leadership and support from Mayor J.L. Edlefsen, Postmaster Harry Yost, Chamber of Commerce President Oscar Worthwine, Walter York and others, the new project moved forward, largely made possible by the Works Progress Administration of the federal government. The WPA, established as part of Franklin Roosevelt's New Deal in 1935, had spent nearly half a million dollars on airport improvements in Idaho by the spring of 1939.[25] The Boise project alone would involve that much federal money before the year was out.

Construction of a new terminal building and moving Varney's 1931 steel drive-through hangar to the bench site took place in 1939. Mayor James L. Straight, who had succeeded J.L. Edlefsen, was featured in an article that appeared in the *Christian Science Monitor* October 19, summarizing Boise's hopes:

"Boise, isolated from large cities and touched by only one railroad, has under construction what is said to be the Nation's largest airport. It is expected that completion of this port will establish Boise as a hub from which feeder lines will radiate in all directions, thus doing much to alleviate the city's isolation."[26] In the years ahead Boise would indeed become the home of a number of feeder lines. In 1939, before the move from the old field, only one intrastate passenger carrier had been in operation. On March 13, 1936, the Idaho Public Utilities Commission had given Capital Air Lines per-

Courtesy Dan Stohr

Planes that flew the mail to Boise for National Airmail Week, 1938, lined up near the United Air Lines hangar at the old field. The new field was begun that year.

mission to haul freight, passengers, and express from Boise to Pocatello, with stops at Burley and Twin Falls. Nampa was added later. The company had only one six-passenger plane at the time, but filled a need, since United flew directly to Salt Lake City, and Boise passengers had to fly there first, then back to Pocatello on National Parks Airways.[27]

Before 1939, North Idaho passengers could fly only out of Spokane, first with Mamer Flying Service. Then, after Walter Varney got the contract from Commercial Air Mail 32 (C.A.M. 32), effective in September, 1929, he was able to fly mail and passengers on a route that included Spokane-Portland-Seattle. Northwest Air Lines reached Spokane and the Pacific Northwest in 1933. The company had begun flying passengers from Minneapolis/St. Paul to Chicago in 1927, but always closed down for the winter. In 1928 a gradual expansion westward was begun, city by city, with Seattle as the eventual terminus. The company's planes only flew over Idaho's panhandle, but offered the area's best connection with the east. Through the years Idaho passengers flew in a variety of Northwest equipment, from Ford Trimotors to DC3s to jets.[28]

Southern Idaho got passenger service from Varney Air Lines in 1930, and after Varney became part of United Air Lines, has been served by that company ever since. Competing lines would be many in the years ahead, as will be described later, but only United has kept Idaho part of its "friendly skies."

Courtesy Don Duvall

The Douglas DC3 and its cargo carrying variations, C-46 and C-47, revolutionized air transport. Here at Boise Air Terminal in 1953 are an American Flyer DC3, Lake Central C46, Capitol Airways C47, Meteor Air Transport C46, and a United Air Lines DC6 in foreground.

ISHS 76-216.1

The Spirit of St. Louis, *moments after landing at Boise's riverside field, September 4, 1927.*

ISHS 63-87.5

Charles A. Lindbergh thrilled huge crowds upon his arrival in Boise. His shy manner and boyish good looks won over all who met him.

FAMOUS VISITORS VIII

Many of the great names in early aviation history visited Idaho. They were usually greeted with enthusiasm by Chambers of Commerce and public officials, wined and dined, and interviewed by the press. None ever had a warmer welcome than Charles A. Lindbergh received when he landed his *Spirit of St. Louis* in Boise on September 4, 1927.

For two weeks before his arrival the city was busy with preparations, aided by advice from Milburn Kusterer, advance man for the Lindbergh tour of all 48 states, sponsored by the Guggenheim Fund for the Advancement of Commercial Aviation. The rules for local celebrations were quite specific: Boise was allowed from 2 until 3:30 p.m. for welcoming ceremonies, and from 3:30 until 4:30 Lindbergh would make an outdoor speech from a platform equipped with a sound amplification system. At a banquet, to start no later than 7 p.m. the Colonel would speak for no more than 15 minutes, and he absolutely had to be in bed by 9 p.m.

Security regulations included a ban on flying escorts, either military or civilian, and there were to be no other planes on the landing field. A guarded hangar was to be provided for the famous plane where mechanics could check out the engine and refuel.

Crowd control and traffic control were of major concern, and the Idaho National Guard, Boise and Caldwell police departments were mobilized to see that parking was adequate, jams were avoided, and the huge crowd expected did not run onto the field. Many organizations wanted to be part of a big parade but were discouraged from participating, as it would take up too much of the precious time allotted for seeing the great Lindy. The fairgrounds site west of the city was selected for his outdoor speech, since anyplace nearer downtown would be too crowded and have inadequate parking.[1]

Thousands gathered around the municipal airport, restrained by ropes and National Guardsmen, to await the appearance of *Spirit of St. Louis* in the southeastern sky. Other thousands lined the parade route between the airport and fairgrounds. Then, as the anxious multitudes strained their eyes and craned their necks for the first sight of the famous plane, now nearly as hour overdue, "All at once there was heard the roar of a motor, and across the skyline flashed the *Spirit of St. Louis.* As the plane, flying low, circled the barracks field and turned toward the main thoroughfare of the city, a cheer went up from the crowd. Everyone had a good view as it banked and turned above the city and then headed for the airport. It was part of Col. Lindbergh's program to fly over the barracks so that the former service men in the hospital could view the plane."[2]

Parked cars lined the Mountain Home highway for miles, and every vantage point along the bench overlooking the airport. Downtown rooftops were crowded with people. Flags and bunting were everywhere. Store windows were decorated for "Lindy Day." Newspaper ads carried welcome messages and pictures of America's hero, "The Lone Eagle." Hotels were crowded with hundreds of people from eastern Oregon as well as southern Idaho, many of whom had come by train, interurban streetcar or automobile the day before. It was a day people remembered for the rest of their lives.[3]

The next transatlantic fliers to visit Idaho were the Frenchmen Dieudonne Costes and Maurice Bellonte. They were the first men to fly

Courtesy Don Duvall

The famed Ryan _Spirit of St. Louis_ *had no forward windows, as this picture shows. They were eliminated to make more room for gas tanks.*

Governor H.C. Baldridge and Mayor Walter F. Hansen were among dignitaries who greeted Lindy at the Boise field. All wore "Lindy Day" welcome badges.

ISHS 60-85.6

Courtesy Charles F. Hummel

Boise Architect F.C. "Fritz" Hummel took his little boy Charles to see Lindbergh's plane on the evening of September 4, 1927. Fritz had designed the hangar where it was sheltered that night.

Courtesy Charles F. Hummel

Lindy was loaded up with proclamations, plaques, and keys to the city wherever he went. Here he is greeted by officers of the Idaho National Guard and Leo J. Falk. Cols. Frederick C. Hummel and M.G. McConnell are at left.

Courtesy Robert R. Auth

Dieudonne Costes and Maurice Bellonte made the first east to west crossing of the Atlantic Ocean September 1-2, 1930. On September 25, 1930, they landed in Boise while on a good will tour of American cities. Their famous plane, the Question Mark, *was unusual for its short lower wings.*

non-stop from Paris to New York on September 1 and 2, 1930 — a distance of 4,100 miles, the longest non-stop flight over water to that time. Costes had earlier made history by flying from Paris to Brazil, with one stop in West Africa, in 1927. Joseph Le Brix accompanied him on this first aerial crossing of the South Atlantic.[4]

Costes and Bellonte were welcomed in Washington, D.C., by President Herbert Hoover, and then flew to Dallas, Texas, to claim the $25,000 prize offered by millionaire Col. William E. Easterwood for the first one-stop flight — Paris-New York-Dallas.[5] The two then embarked on a month-long good will tour across America.

Although Costes and Bellonte's rigid schedule allowed only a one-hour stop in Boise before they had to continue along the Varney airmail route to Pasco, Portland and Seattle, nearly 10,000 people gathered at the airport to greet them. Governor Baldridge, Mayor Pope and other dignitaries were on hand to make speeches and pose for pictures. Boise High School Latin teacher Evelyn Wenstrom was one of four local fliers who escorted the red Hispano-Suiza biplane *Question Mark* as it appeared over the field.

When the plane rolled to a stop in front of the hangars and the speakers' stand, the band played the French national anthem and the crowd cheered wildly. The pilots stayed in their cockpits while they checked weather reports, and then personally supervised the refueling and servicing of their plane. Only then did they allow themselves to be led to the platform for the official welcome. No sooner had they started in that direction than a swarm of small boys rushed out of the crowd toward the *Question Mark*. "Then the volatile French excitement came to the surface. To Costes, self-evidently, the *Question Mark* is only a little more precious than his right eye, and seeing the onrush, he turned quickly, shouting in purest French: 'Will everybody please kindly get away from there quick?' It was as near as the more courteous French could get to that famous American admonition 'Get the hell out of there'." Dr. P.G. Germen, staff physician at the U.S. Veterans Hospital, acted as interpreter during the Governor's speech and Costes' response.

The visitors had lunch at the Airways Inn beside the field, but without much privacy, as the eager crowd pressed noses to the windows to watch. They were shooed away by police. "Those two Frenchmen were too polite to say anything about the absence of what to most Frenchmen is an indispensable part of their lunch — vin rouge. It is barely possible that they don't drink vin, but not probable," observed a *Statesman* reporter.[6]

Among U.S. Army Air Corps aviators who visited Boise and other Idaho towns early, many had made records that would stand as landmarks in air history. We have earlier mentioned the exploits of Albert W. Stevens, balloonist who set world records for parachuting and altitude in the 1920s and '30s. He and pilot John A. Macready were in Idaho several times in the Twenties. Macready had records of his own, most notably the first non-stop flight, New York to San Diego in 1923, with Oakley G. Kelley. For this and other pioneering achievements he was inducted into the Aviation Hall of Fame at Dayton, Ohio. Carl A. Spaatz, who commanded the 1919 Victory Loan Flying Circus that came to Pocatello and Boise, is another Hall of Famer, especially for his leadership in World War II. In 1929 he and Ira Eaker set a new world's endurance record in an army plane that refueled in mid-air.

Navy flier Walter Hinton, pilot of the U.S. Navy's famed NC-4 seaplane, that became the first airplane to fly the Atlantic in 1919, was in Boise on May 13 and 14, 1931. He was sponsored by the National Exchange Clubs on a coast-to-coast tour to promote aviation. He spoke to the local Exchange Club and to 1,500 "breathlessly attentive" students at Boise High School. He described the flight of NC-1, NC-3, and NC-4 in their daring assault on the Atlantic. His NC-4 was the only one of the three to complete the journey. He also told of his adventures in charting the Amazon jungles of Brazil with Captain A.W. Stevens. When reminded by a reporter that Stevens had lived in Idaho for several years, Hinton praised him as "one of the ablest, most resourceful fliers and photographers" he had ever known. Hinton was scheduled for stops in Emmett, Mountain Home and Pocatello en route to Salt Lake City.[7] Other famous visitors of 1931 were Charles and Anne Morrow Lindbergh who landed briefly at Nampa for refueling. (See page 83.)

Sir Hubert Wilkins, noted British explorer of north and south polar regions, visited Boise on January 8, 1932. On April 16, 1928, Wilkins had flown from Point Barrow, Alaska, to Spitzbergen, Norway — the first trans-Arctic flight with an airplane. (Two dirigible airships had done it earlier.) He had recently attempted a submarine trip under the polar ice, and local reporters plied him with questions about that effort and what caused its mechanical failure. He had hoped to use the submarine *Nautilus* to set up and supply a weather station in the Arctic as an aid to navigation for aircraft. Lack of good weather prediction was a serious handicap, and source of danger to the fliers of the 1920s and '30s. Wilkins told newsmen that he had been acquainted with A.A. Bennett, Idaho commercial pilot, in Alaska several years before. Bennett, later director of Idaho's aeronautics division, had flown in Alaska for six years and was one of its earliest bush pilots. For all his fame as a flier, Sir Hubert's visit to Boise was made in a regularly scheduled Varney Air Lines Boeing 40-B passenger plane.[8] (In 1932 Varney was a division of United, but still kept its own identity.)

In June, 1932, Captain Lewis A. Yancey showed Idaho an aviation novelty when he flew an autogiro into Boise airport. Yancey's claim to fame was a 1929 flight from New York to Rome as navigator for pilot Roger Q. Williams. The autogiro, often called a "windmill plane" because of its four rotor blades, was a pioneer version of the helicopter. Yancey had flown his unusual aircraft in South America, had landed in Yosemite National Park, and skirted the walls of Crater Lake, Oregon. He also held several speed records, but not in an autogiro. Yancey's sponsor on his cross-country tour was a spark plug manufacturer. Yancey claimed to have set a new "world's record" while in Boise, when he took a three-year-old boy for a spin — his youngest passenger yet. He apparently found some parents with a lot of faith in the odd-looking autogiro.[9]

Clyde Pangborn, who made the first non-stop flight across the Pacific from Tokyo to Wenatchee in 1931, landed in Pocatello on May 3, 1933, en route from Seattle to New York City. He was carrying Chinese officials to a meeting with President Franklin D. Roosevelt. Pangborn, as noted in Chapter IV, had begun his flying career in St. Maries, Idaho.[10]

In later years other air celebrities would touch down at Idaho airports as passenger aviation became commonplace. We have mentioned just a few who attracted wide attention in those pioneering days, before we became blasé about flying. Today we might happen to see famous politicians, movie stars, or musicians in any of our airports any day of the week, but they usually come unheralded. Unlike the early heroes of aviation they rarely draw cheering thousands, or have parades organized in their honor.

Courtesy Boise Public Library

Women members of Boise Flying Club did much of the work on the organization's social and fund-raising functions.

Courtesy Doris Willy Crowder

Boise chapter of Associated Women Pilots was instrumental in organizing an "Airathon," held June 30, 1941. Kneeling are Doris Willy and Mayor James L. Straight; standing are Margaret Loy, Francis Sale and Helen Beck Higby.

WOMEN IN IDAHO SKIES IX

The first woman to pilot an airplane in Idaho was barnstormer Alys McKey. She took off from Boise fairgrounds in a Curtiss biplane on May 30, 1913, at a time when very few American women had flown.[1] When former Boise business woman Volara Romanza Nelson died in an automobile crash in Nebraska in July, 1921, newspaper accounts said she was the first female pilot licensed by the Aero Club of America. Since many women were flying by 1921, this may indicate only that licensing was not widely practiced yet. In any case, Mrs. Nelson, originally from Rupert, is the first Idaho woman recorded as a flier.[2]

In the summer of 1927, Art Walters and his wife Dorothy took the train to Troy, Ohio, where they bought a new "deluxe" Waco Ten biplane for use in his flying school in Boise. He had used Curtiss Jennies for the first year, so this was a big step forward for the young company. Dorothy Walters rode in the forward cockpit and read the maps for her husband as they flew across the country with the new plane. She took the controls part of the way home while her husband gave her instruction by hand signals. A reporter who interviewed her wrote, "She is entirely unimpressed with the danger in flying, declaring that it is much safer in the air than on the highways. A plane, she says, is much easier to control than an automobile." Dorothy Walters predicted that flying would become a very popular sport among women. "Of course they will fly," she said. "Why not? There's nothing more thrilling in the world."[3]

An all male Boise Flying Club, started in late 1927, soon had women demanding a chance to join and to receive lessons. "They express perfect willingness to go through with the ground school work on motors, rigging and other mechanical features if only they can get into the air," reported the *Idaho Statesman* on March 9, 1928. "Directors have taken the matter under advisement for 30 days, and in the meantime advise the would be aviatrices to send their applications to Henry A. Hardt, club secretary." Fred Kopke, club president, said "The desire of Boise women to fly is a very real thing."[4]

On April 19, 1928, Boise Flying Club's directors voted to accept women as members, although, as the *Statesman* reported, the club had been "formed for men and intended for men. But when pinned down to good reasons why women shouldn't fly, the directors were soon muddled . . ."[5] In the so-called "Roaring Twenties," men were still getting used to the idea that the "flappers" of the post-war era were not going to be shut out of any enjoyable and exciting activity just because they were still though of as the "frailer sex" and in need of protection. In fairness to the men, in this case they gave in without a struggle — despite one old bachelor who suggested (facetiously) that women should submit their photographs with their applications for membership.[6] Boise Flying Club proved it was not sexist, just as it had earlier proved that it was not racist. Chinese Dr. Wing Lee had been an active member of the club since its founding. In March, 1928, he bought a 230 horsepower radial engine and allowed the club to use it for study purposes before it was installed in the plane he was planning to buy.

Tex Rankin of Portland addressed the club on May 9, 1928, and announced plans to open a Boise branch of his noted flying school. He encouraged Idaho women to sign up for lessons, and said that 12 "girls" were enrolled in his Portland school. "Their records in some phases of the work outrank those of the men," he declared.[8] There were several women in Boise Flying club's first class of 25, taught by Russell Owen, pilot for sheepman Jock Brockie. They decided to wear all white flying costumes. Owen, who had gained a reputation as "Idaho's sheep herding aviator" promised to teach his students all of the tricks he had learned in several years of landing in Idaho's mountains and deserts.[9]

In August, 1928, Aldene Grupe was part of a family team that started an aviation school at Lewiston. She had more than 600 hours of flying experience at the time, dating from a trip with her father when she was only 10 years old, and had served as his navigator on a flight over Idaho's mountains from Laurel, Montana, to Pasco, Washington. The papers called her "a modern Ruth Elder," even though nobody had heard of Elder before she attempted to fly the Atlantic with a male co-pilot only the year before. That flight ended with a forced landing in the ocean near the Azores Islands where the two fliers were rescued by a Dutch tanker. Ruth Elder went on to become one of America's best known female pilots, and something of a glamour girl. Her flight and subsequent fame led to a fashion for "Ruth ribbons" of the kind she used to fasten her hair — not unlike the headbands tennis stars wear today.[11]

Stories of national and international women fliers like Ruth Elder, Francis Grayson and Amelia Earhart, and local girls like Dorothy Walters, certainly fanned an interest in flying among Idaho women. Evelyn Wenstrom, who taught Latin at Boise High School, made her first solo flight in May, 1930. "Miss Wenstrom made a perfect take-off, circled the city and surrounding country and settled on the field in a perfect landing. Her plane for the solo flight was the Travelair biplane of the Flying Service," reported the *Evening Capital News.* Like other fliers at the time, she helped support her hobby by flying passengers when she could.[12]

On September 25, 1930,[13] Wenstrom was one of four local pilots who convoyed famous French aviators Costes and Bellonte into Boise. "I was thrilled almost to tears by the trip," she said, describing what it was like to be part of a four-plane flight of local aviators escorting Costes and Bellonte's famed "Question Mark." The two Frenchmen had flown non-stop from Paris to New York a few weeks earlier and were on a good will tour of the United States.

Mrs. Rollin Scott of Nampa, who began flying lessons at Nampa with Bill Pons in November, 1929, was flying solo in July, 1930. "Imagine one of Nampa's popular young society matrons up in the air soaring through space, directing a modern airplane with the same composure that most folks direct their autos," gushed the *Capital News.* Asked if a flight did not make her nervous, she said, "I must confess that I am not without fear, but my fear adds to my cautiousness and to carefulness in watching the mechanism of my machine. I realize that something may go wrong. One wants to keep one's head, you know."[14]

Despite the fact that Mrs. Scott and at least one other Idaho woman were flying in 1930, newspapers continued to write about Evelyn Wenstrom as "Idaho's only woman pilot." In April, 1931, she made headlines by flying her single-seat Aeronca monoplane to Spokane to attend a meeting of the Inland Empire Education Association. When she took off from Clarkston on the way to Moscow, she ran into a 60-mile an hour wind that buffeted her plane wildly and pushed it 20 miles up the Clearwater valley, away from the course she wanted to fly. Her sister Ruth, riding in a companion plane flown by Clarence Savage, was taken from his ship "almost unconscious from air sickness," after both planes managed to land safely at Lewiston. It was Ruth's first flight. Far from being afraid, Evelyn said the experience had given her confidence. "I feel that I am able to cope with most any sort of conditions now."[15]

When the Pacific Northwest States Air Tour came to Nampa in late June, 1931, women pilots were a big part of the show. Dorothy Hester, Florence Lowe, and Gladys O'Donnell were the headliners, along with old timers Tex Rankin and Nick Mamer. Echoing a sentiment often heard from these early women, Virginia Ogden said, "I'm crazy about flying. I've been flying about two years and I think it is much safer than driving an auto. I wouldn't think of driving a car over the highway we followed." Dora Skinner, a Yakima doctor's wife, left a three-year-old daughter at home to fly in the big meet.[16]

The most famous female flyer to visit Idaho in 1931 was Anne Morrow Lindbergh. She and husband Charles stopped briefly in Nampa for refueling on October 22, 1931. They were on their way home from Seattle, called back from a tour of the Orient by the death of Mrs. Lindbergh's father, Senator Dwight W. Morrow. While the famous couple were in Nampa, hundreds who had gathered at Boise for a welcoming ceremony waited in vain. Understandably, the Lindberghs were in no mood for celebrations or crowds. A reporter who happened to be in Nampa interviewed the two, thereby scoring a scoop over his Boise rivals. Lindy explained that they had no fixed schedule, but only wanted to get to New York as soon as possible. Anne Lindbergh was eager to see their baby, Charles, Jr., from whom they had been separated for several months.[17] This was the child the Lindberghs would lose when he was kidnapped and murdered on March 1, 1932 — a tragedy the grieving young couple never quite got over.[18]

A new career in aviation for women opened in May, 1930, when eight nurses were hired by Boeing Air Transport to work as stewardesses on the San Francisco-Chicago Run. Steve Stimpson, Boeing's San Francisco manager, proposed the idea to his bosses in Seattle in the belief that having young women aboard to assist passengers was good psychology — it would be backed up by the nurses' training in case of accident or air sickness. (The latter qualification for stewardesses would not be advertised to the public, of course). Ellen Church, head of that first group of airline stewardesses, was an Iowa girl who had received her nursing training in Minnesota and was working in San Francisco. It was she who persuaded Stimpson to propose the idea to his superiors. She had always wanted to fly and had taken lessons before going into nursing.[19]

Helen Taylor of Weiser was one of the first Idaho women to become a stewardess for United Air Lines after that company was formed

Courtesy Robert R. Auth

Mrs. Walter Varney and daughter Virginia traveled in style in 1928 in this Varney Breese monoplane.

through the merger of Boeing Air Transport, Varney Air Lines, Pacific Air Transport, and National Air Transport. She worked on the new Boeing 247s that landed regularly at Boise on the Portland to Salt Lake City run in 1934.[20] This first really modern airliner carried 10 passengers, two pilots, and a stewardess. Many Idaho women would enter this new field of aviation in the years ahead, and the qualifications and training changed dramatically. Nursing training was not a requirement after the first few years, but fierce competition for the jobs gave college women an edge. For a long time strict height and weight limits were imposed, and a woman who married was forced to resign. With the sheer numbers of young women who wanted to be stewardesses, a glamour profession from the beginning, it is small wonder that airlines chose only the prettiest and the brightest for many years.[21]

The uniforms the first stewardesses wore were practical but unattractive — baggy caps that covered most of their heads, apparently to save hairdos from wind and prop wash, dark green jersey double-breasted jackets, longish skirts, and very long capes. What Steve Stimpson wanted, he wrote in a memo, was "not at all the flapper type girl."[22] In the next few years, however, uniforms changed with frequency. The image created by the new style-conscious outfits was of crisp professionalism, with a hint of the military. It may have been America's rush

Courtesy Boise City Archives

Boise Municipal Airport shortly before the move to the new bench location. Old channels of Boise River are clearly visible as dark swaths, lower left.

to prepare to defend itself in the event the country was drawn into the European war that Hitler launched on September 1, 1939, or it may have started earlier, but the uniforms of stewardesses became increasingly trim, tailored and military. Shorter skirts, seamed stockings, and high heels certainly kept these young women from looking less than feminine, even in uniform styles that required shirts and neckties.

Although United Air Lines had been flying 21-passenger DC3 Mainliners on the Portland to Salt Lake run over Idaho since 1937, the planes could not land safely at Boise's little riverside field. Not until January 21, 1939, when the city's new airport south of town was ready, did the first DC3 touch down there. Carmen Laragan of Hagerman, the only Idaho-born stewardess on the United staff at the time, was scheduled to serve on the inaugural flight, as was veteran airmail pilot Walter E. "Doc" Eefsen, now chief pilot on the Portland-Salt Lake City run. Eefsen's Boise connections were important, since he had been stationed there for several years while flying the mail for Varney Air Lines.[33]

Since Boise's airport was socked in by freezing fog that week, most of the ceremonies planned for the big day had to be canceled. When the first DC3 Mainliner did land, it was nearly 10 p.m. Fog had prevented the scheduled morning landing and the westbound plane had flown on past the city, but the skies were clear when the evening plane from Portland landed before "500 half-frozen spectators." The welcoming reception was jubilant, despite the change in plans, and lots of pictures were taken of stewardess Eva Kidrick and pilots Eddie Garbutt and Guy Cain.[24]

Stewardesses got a new challenge on the trans-Idaho run May 1, 1939, when DC3 sleeper service was inaugurated.[25] Some of the 21-seat DC3s had been converted to Pullman-style berths for 7 passengers. A man who flew regularly between Portland and New York described what it was like:

"When it was parked on the runway you walked 'uphill' to the front seats. There were seven rows of seats: a single row of seats on the left, and two rows of seats on the right. The right hand seats converted into seven beds, parallel to the aisle. They were quite hard for the stewardesses to make up — pushing and pulling levers, etc., so the passengers often helped. Obviously the sleeper version limited passenger capacity to 14 on overnight flights and we hoped the seven left hand seats weren't all filled so we'd have a place to sit awhile before going to bed.

"By the time we landed at Boise airport, most of us were already in bed whether we wanted to be or not. The plane taxied into one side of the hangar to unload, load and refuel, and then out the other side. We could lie in bed and look out the window at people walking around in the hangar admiring our 'dreadnought of the skies'!" (The drive-through hangar referred to was the one Walter Varney had built at the old riverside field in 1931, on what is now the campus of Boise State University. It was taken apart and moved to the new airport in May, 1939).

"Since the DC3s were not pressurized, the stewardesses asked us when we retired if we wanted to be wakened before landings so we could adjust for change in pressure by holding our noses and blowing. We always did. And — it was always nice to have a pretty young girl (as I recall) wake us several times."[26]

Preparedness for national defense became a major concern in 1939 after World War II started in Europe. Women interested in flying were affected most directly by the establishment of Civilian Pilot Training programs at Idaho colleges and universities. Even earlier, the federal government had begun to fund aeronautics training, aimed at preparing the enormous number of fliers the nation would need if war came. The Civil Aeronautics Authority, in explaining the new programs, said that "only by such an approach can the United States safeguard itself against the vast aerial militarization now being pressed with fanatical zeal by foreign powers."[27]

Courtesy Boise City Archives

Many Idaho women learned to fly in the years before Pearl Harbor -- some in the CPT program, others through private clubs.

CPT programs were instituted at the University of Idaho, The College of Idaho, U. of I. Southern Branch (later Idaho State), and Boise Junior College. Women students were eligible for the courses, and eagerly joined as soon as they were offered. Joyce Whitmore, a College of Idaho coed, wrote a series of newspaper features for the *Idaho Statesman* while in pilot training at the Caldwell school, and later an "Aviation in Boise Valley" column. These informative, light-hearted, and gossipy articles are a rich source of material on the campuses and airports of southwest Idaho and eastern Oregon in the months before Pearl Harbor. She describes vividly her own adventures learning to fly. Here is a sample — her first tailspin:

"The little ship lost speed and hung there in a stall, then — wheel back and hard rudder and suddenly the sky was gone and below me was the flat saucer like earth, wheeling ponderously around the nose. My head hit the cockpit ceiling as the ship dropped from under me and I rose against the safety belt. I gasped frantically to relieve the pressure change in my eardrums. My knees went wobbly, and I was a frightened gal. White Lake Lowell swung round the horizon once — twice — and then I felt the controls move and the little plane quivered all over as it met the solid impact of air and straightened out into normal flight.

"Why that's fun! Suddenly it occurred to me that the feeling was just like that of a breathtaking roller-coaster drop, and with difficulty I suppressed a whoop of joy. I wanted to do it again."[28] Joyce was the only woman in that first class of CPT students at The College of Idaho. She got her pilot's license on May 12, 1940.[29]

Twelve days later Congress passed, by a vote of 391 to 1 a bill approving President Franklin D. Roosevelt's plan for expansion of the Army Air Corps and a broad plan to train 50,000 pilots. Programs in operation that were training 2,500 pilots annually were authorized to train 8,500.[30] Harry Morrison of Boise immediately urged city and county officials and the Chamber of Commerce to push for federal assistance to establish expanded military aviation facilities. "Boise and the entire Boise valley offer an ideal location for establishment of training headquarters for all classes of military airplanes," he said.[31] The quotas announced in June, 1940, were for the training of 600 college and 120 non-college fliers in Montana, Idaho, Oregon and Washington. Boise Junior College president Eugene Chaffee announced that his school would train 30 that summer. The College of Idaho also participated in the "authorized summer emergency program."[32] Women who had been trained and now had their licenses became instructors in the Civilian Pilot Training program. Irene Crane of Kellogg was hired to teach a class of CPT students at the University of Idaho in September, 1940, shortly after she received her commercial pilot's license and instructor's rating. She was working for a degree in mechanical engineering when she learned to fly.

Courtesy Doris Willy Crowder

Doris Willy was secretary of Boise Associated Women Pilots when this picture was taken to publicize the club's annual dance, May 3, 1941.

"Her students, dubious at first at the prospect of a woman instructor, and one of their fellow students . . . changed their minds after their first flight with her at the controls. Their highest praise for her is 'She knows her stuff.'" Rachel Swayne of Nampa and Beulah Keister of Murray were women students in Crane's class.[33]

Many women who learned to fly in the late '30s and early '40s were not part of federal programs, however, They learned through local flying clubs that had bought planes for shared use. They had frequent fundraisers, both to buy new equipment, and for the social pleasures they offered. The Idaho Pilots Association had branch chapters in Boise, Twin Falls, Idaho Falls and Pocatello in 1940.[34] There were only seven licensed women pilots in the state at that time, but they organized their own club, the Associated Women Pilots of Idaho. Members wore neat uniforms with chevrons on the sleeves under which were displayed patches indicating Red Cross Certificates, radio licenses, and flying licenses earned.[35] Women were also active in local chapters of the Idaho Pilots Association, and took the lead in organizing the Boise chapter's statewide "Airathon" held June 30, 1940. Elaine Hunt was president of the Boise chapter, Associated Women Pilots then. She and members Margaret Loy, Doris Willey, Betty Nicholas, Frances Sale and Irene Dunne flew to Seattle for the fourth annual meeting of national AWP. Hunt was the only Idaho woman at the time to hold a Limited Commercial License, and was flying passengers regularly for Webb's Flying Service."[36]

The Idaho women at the 1940 national convention of AWP in Seattle made a big hit. Margaret Loy of New Plymouth was elected vice president, Lucille Johnston, secretary, and Doris Willey and Irene Dunne were placed on the nominating committee for the 1941 meeting to be held in Spokane.[37]

The first Idaho state Airathon, organized by the Idaho Pilots Association, was held in Boise on June 30, 1940. Aviation safety was the theme, as fliers from all over the state gathered for a program of stunts and contests. Betty Nicholas was first and Margaret Loy second in the spot landing contest for women.[38]

A few women continued to enroll in Civilian Pilot Training programs in Idaho colleges in the summer of 1940. Joey Hedden was the only woman in Northwest Nazarene College's course, taught by Allen Platt. Katherine Tuller was the lone coed in The College of Idaho program. Bettina Kroeger, Jean Schooler and Jacqueline Millar of Boise were enrolled at Boise Junior College.[39] In September, 1940, Joyce Whitmore, who had learned to fly in The College of Idaho CPT program, was one of three pilots who flew new Porterfield 65s 1,500 miles from Kansas City to Caldwell. The trip took two and a half days with frequent landings for fuel.[40]

Laura Ingalls, "ace stunt flyer" from Burbank, California, landed in Boise on October 2, 1940, and gave flying for women a further boost. She had flown in an air show in Boise in 1938 before becoming known for aerial acrobatics. Now her statements were eagerly quoted by the papers. "Why, every woman wants to fly — even mothers. Anyone with any imagination loves the idea of getting 'way up in the clouds, where time and distance are eliminated, and earthly pettiness forgotten." She told listeners that flying was still a man's field, but that women could earn men's respect for their abilities. With the rapid expansion of the CPT programs nationwide, she thought women pilots had an excellent opportunity to become instructors. (At least two in Idaho already were). Laura Ingalls flew from New York to California in 1935 in 18 hours and 10 minutes. She was the first woman to fly solo across the country, and her later non-stop flight was still the best for either men or women, and 5-1/2 hours faster than Amelia Earhart's. She said she preferred long distance flying to stunting but had to do it to make a living.[41]

A blow to the hopes of would-be women pilots came in an order from the CAA in late October, 1940. No women would be allowed to enroll in advanced commercial flying courses. The one woman in the Boise Junior College course was "automatically dropped from the list."[42] The nation's drive to train 50,000 pilots was increasingly concerned with the need for fighter and bomber fliers. The Battle of Britain, the three-month air war over southeast England, in which RAF Spitfires had outfought the Luftwaffe and discouraged Hitler from attempt-

Courtesy Gene Nora Jessen

Three of the most famous women pilots of all time are in this 1930s group of Ninety-Nines. Front row, far right: Amelia Earhart, with trophy; Amy Mollison and Ruth Nichols.

ing an invasion, had clearly shown American military planners the enormous loss of planes and pilots to be expected in modern aerial combat. There seemed no place in such a war for women, who had never been considered for combat duty at any time.[43]

Once the United States joined the war, however, the tremendous resource of skilled women pilots could not be ignored. Famed long distance and speed flier Jackie Cochran had pushed for a women's flying service to ferry Lockhead Hudson bombers to Britain, authorized by Congress with the Lend Lease Act of March, 1941. Civilian pilots hired to ferry the planes to England from Canada threatened to go on strike if women were allowed to do "man's work." A Compromise was worked out allowing Jackie Cochran to fly one of the big bombers across the Atlantic, but only if a man took off and landed. (Cochran had already demonstrated in 60 practice takeoffs and landings that she could do it smoothly.) Eventually she was allowed to recruit American women pilots to fly for the British Air Transport Auxiliary — a service that ferried thousands of planes of all kinds during the war.[44]

After America went to war, two flying services for women were established — the Women's Auxiliary Ferrying Squadron (WAFS) and the Women's Airforce Service Pilots (WASP). They flew every kind of military aircraft the armed forces had — often to the resentment of men who felt that piloting hot fighters and big bombers could not possibly be done by frail women. The women were sometimes embarrassed by this too, since most of them didn't really want to show the boys up.[45]

Women were also enrolled in the Civil Air Patrol, organized in 1942 to augment the war effort of the military by flying search and rescue and other missions. One Idaho assignment, kept top secret at the time, was patrolling mountain forests for fires started by Japanese incendiary balloons, released in great numbers during the war to create panic and disruption of services in western states.[46]

A national organization for female fliers had been organized on November 2, 1929, on Long Island, New York. Amelia Earhart was elected first president in 1931. The group took the name "Ninety-Nines," because that was the number of charter members.[47] The Idaho chapter of the Ninety-Nines was formed on October 15, 1954, at Boise, and an Eastern Idaho chapter October 14, 1956. Members were from Wyoming, as well as from several Idaho towns.[48] North Idaho women were affiliated with a Spokane chapter.

Perhaps Idaho's most colorful and best known female pilot in 1991 is Gladys Buroker who flies out of Silverwood, north of Coeur d'Alene. She learned to fly in September, 1932, in a Waco 10 with an OX 5 engine. She once parachuted into a University of Idaho football game, but her jumping with a barnstorming group ended when she injured a knee. During the Civilian Pilot Training program, Gladys taught men to fly at St. Martin's College near Olympia, Washington. "I have been very well received by the men in aviation from the beginning," she declared to an interviewer. During the war Gladys and husband Herb Buroker moved their flying operation to Weeks Field at Coeur d'Alene where she taught students to fly seven days a week, often 12 to 14 hours a day. She recalls stunt flying with the great Tex Rankin and Dave Rahm. Of her ride with Rankin she said "Anyone who tells you that you can't do acrobatics in an Ercoupe is mistaken. He could snap roll it and slow roll it, he could do anything with it." Over a long career in aviation Gladys Buroker has flown about every kind of plane, taught her own children and grandchildren to fly, ridden a motorcycle across the country, parachuted 17 times, become a registered nurse, and is now flying her own hot air balloon. She has become a role model for young women who aspire to careers in aviation, for the women who pioneered the skies proved long ago that they could do anything with an airplane that men could do.[49]

An Idaho woman was one of 13 out of a select group of 25 who passed the physical in a female astronaut research program at Lovelace Clinic in Albuquerque in 1961. Gene Nora Jessen, then a flight instructor at the University

Courtesy Gladys Buroker

Top: Gladys Buroker soloed on September 24, 1932, the day this picture was taken.
Above: Buroker with her first motorcycle, a four-cylinder Indian Ace, 1933.

Courtesy Gene Nora Jessen

Gene Nora Jessen of Boise. She was honored with election as President, International Ninety-Nines, and served 1988-1990. She also wrote a significant history of the organization.

of Oklahoma, and later a leader in Idaho aviation circles, successfully completed a rigorous series of tests (designed for men) at a time when a program for female astronauts was only being considered. When word of the testing got out, opposition and controversy rapidly developed, even including a Congressional investigation. The program was scrapped. It was only a temporary set-back, however, and eventually female astronauts were included. Jessen later wrote of her experience, "My only disappointment was in having my finger jerked prematurely out of the pie. However, my nature does not allow me to fight for purely female causes. So often feminists are self-defeating and unhappy people."[50]

Although an Idaho woman has yet to be rocketed into space, Barbara Morgan of McCall was one of the ten chosen for NASA's Teacher in Space program. She trained with the crew of the ill-fated *Challenger* space shuttle in which fellow teacher Christa McCauliffe perished with the rest when its rocket exploded shortly after takeoff on January 28, 1986. Morgan has been active in space education nationally in the years since her involvement with *Challenger*. It might have been she who took that fatal flight. She is still, in July, 1991, the "Teacher in Space designee," scheduled to fly next when the program is resumed.[51]

Delfina Aldecoa of Boise was the first woman Air Traffic Control tower chief in the Pacific Northwest. She held posts in Great Falls, Boise and Spokane before serving as chief at Hillsboro, Oregon.

Courtesy Delfina Aldecoa

Courtesy Gene Nora Jessen

When Governor Cecil Andrus proclaimed Idaho Women in Aviation Week, Ann Stott and Gene Nora Jessen were there for the signing.

Courtesy Chet Moulton

Boise has changed a lot since women pilots first flew into the riverside field in the 1930s. Left: Maxine McClellan, early Idaho pilot.

Courtesy NASA

Barbara Morgan of McCall is Idaho's Teacher in Space and next to fly.

Courtesy Gladys Buroker

Courtesy Gladys Buroker

Courtesy Gladys Buroker

Above: Mark Semich and Gladys Buroker in a Semco balloon.
Top right: Fokker "Red Baron" triplane flown by Gladys Buroker at Athol, Idaho.
Middle right: Gladys with a Ryan B1.

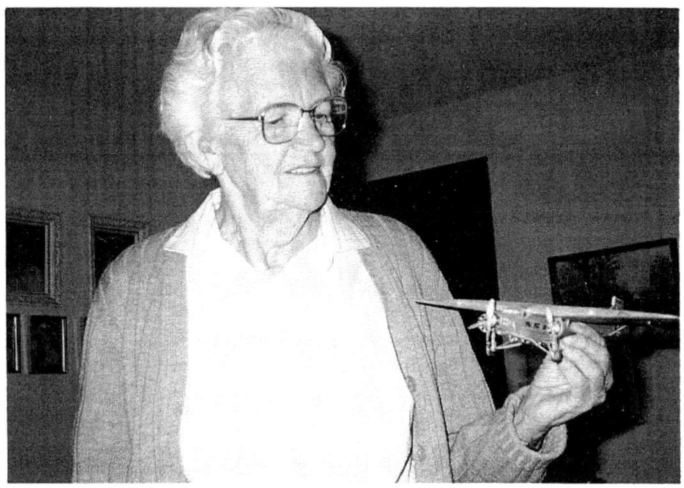

Courtesy Idaho Department of Aeronautics

Gladys Buroker in July, 1991, with a model Ford Trimotor, one of the many kinds of planes she has flown.

IDAHO STATE AERONAUTICS X

The Idaho State Aeronautics Department was created in 1929 as an Aeronautics Division in the State Department of Public Works. Arthur C. Blomgren, with the title "Airways Engineer" was its first head. The 1929 legislature also passed a series of acts to enable the new division to carry out its responsibilities, described in general terms as "for the purpose of establishing a state policy of constructive cooperation in aviation development." Most important of the new laws were those authorizing cities, counties and highway districts to acquire lands not to exceed 640 acres for maintaining and operating airports, authorizing the issuance of bonds or the levy of taxes for such purposes, and establishing a $25,000 aeronautics fund, to be maintained by a tax on aviation fuel and license fees for planes.[1]

In his first biennial report to the governor, Arthur Blomgren noted that the number of airports in the state had grown from six, before the Idaho Air Commerce Act of 1929 was passed, to 38 at the end of 1930. Cities and towns had been quick to take advantage of their new authority to submit bond issues to the voters to get airports built or improved. Of the six airfields in existence before 1929, two were condemned as inadequate under new safety standards, meaning that in reality 34 new fields had been built and approved in less than two years. Coeur d'Alene, which had purchased land for an airport in 1916, had Idaho's earliest municipal field and one of the first in the country.[2]

In May, 1931, the State Board of Examiners approved purchase of a state airplane. Engineer Blomgren, who was a pilot, had testified that the plane was necessary for travel of state officials "where speed is required." In June, 1931, a $4,835 Travelair was ordered. Its specifications were: three-place open biplane with two-seat forward cockpit; top speed, 120 miles per hour; cruising speed, 100 miles per hour; range, 600 miles; to be able to take off with heavy loads in 400 feet.[3]

Blomgren flew the plane regularly in 1931-32. He organized and took part in an Intermountain Air Tour in July, 1932, that involved most of the well-known pilots of Idaho, eastern Washington, and western Montana. The list of participants and their planes is like a hall of fame of pioneer aviation in the region: Bill Bales, Lewiston, in a Great Lakes; Virgil Adair, Lewiston, a Challenger Robin; Bob Johnson, Missoula, a Standard; Gordon Moore, Nampa, a Fleet; George Perry, Nampa, a Stearman; A.A. Bennett, Boise, a Zenith; Bob King, Boise, a Fairchild; Nick Mamer, Spokane, a Stearman; Frank Colthorp, Boise, a Bull Pup; F.H. Christensen, Pocatello, a Fokker Universal; Ralph Knapp, Pocatello, a Stinson; Art Sevenson, Pocatello, a Warner Waco, and Bill Hanmer, Salmon, a Barling.[4] Mamer and Perry withdrew before the tour started because of other commitments, but Dick Johnson of Missoula, brother of Bob, flew Johnson Flying Service's Standard.

In races held in Boise to kick off the goodwill tour, A.A. Bennett in his Wasp-powered Zenith narrowly beat out Art Blomgren in the state's smaller Travelair.[5] Stormy weather messed up the schedule and caused Blomgren to ground loop the Travelair at Missoula, forcing him out of the tour until repairs were made. Virgil Adair did spectacular stunt flying at Coeur d'Alene, despite high winds. By then only six planes were still on the tour.[6]

The state airplane flew 40,440 miles in its

first 18 months, at a net cost of 7.49 cents per mile. This compared favorably with the 8 cents per mile paid for automobile travel, but did not prevent partisan politics from getting involved over the cost of having a state plane at all. In that 18 months the Aeronautics Division had received $42,853 in revenues and spent $35,058 — more than $20,500 of it for airport improvements. The crunch of the Great Depression was already being felt, but Idaho's legislators, along with their constituents, had at least a mild case of aviation fever. That would cool off fast as times got worse.[7] With Democrat C. Ben Ross in the governor's chair, the Republicans naturally attacked the state's ownership of a plane as an extravagance the governor himself never used (although that was not its purpose). Citing early claims that the state airplane would result in savings, Republican chairman R.P. Parry sarcastically suggested that if the state were to buy 502 new planes at a cost of $4,835 apiece, the savings would amount to millions.[8] 1932 was an election year, of course, and such attacks were part of the game. On November 1, the day of the election, another attack was launched involving use of the state airplane. Governor Ross was accused of having sent the plane on a "joy ride" in April when the state game warden flew to Washington, D.C., to present President Herbert Hoover with a nonresident fish and game license. "The cost of this 'joy ride' was $310 and at this particular time hundreds of deer and elk were dying from starvation within a few miles of the state game warden's office," charged the head of a sportsmen's group. "The $300 spent on this trip would have bought some 30 tons of hay, which would have kept hundreds of deer alive."[9] The attack had little effect, and Ross and the Democrats won in a landslide.

As the depression worsened, aviation in Idaho suffered along with other activities. The 1935 legislature appropriated no money to the aeronautics division other than what could be collected from licensing fees and the five cents per gallon fuel tax. Between January 1, 1935, and October 31, 1936, this amounted to only $12,035. Total payroll for the division was $4,259. W.R. Graham, now Director of Aeronautics, in his biennial report to Governor Ross, pointed out that it was exceedingly difficult to carry out the provisions of Chapter 197 of the 1929 Session Laws with only the money collected from these two sources. The Great Depression had reduced the number of licensed planes in the state from 52 in 1931 to only 28 in 1932 and 33 in 1933, thereby cutting the amount collected on licensing and the fuel tax proportionately.[10] The number of airfields had continued to increase, however, to 57 by October 31, 1936. Many of the newest, like that at Idaho Falls, had been assisted by W.P.A. projects — one of the reasons the legislature felt it could eliminate a state appropriation to the department.

Ed M. Bryan was director in the biennium ending December 3, 1938. The division was still operating solely on gasoline tax and licensing money, with no additional appropriation from the legislature. Salaries were virtually the same as in 1936 — a total of $4,537.50 for the director and his office staff. The division no longer had an airplane in 1938 and Bryan recommended the purchase of one for the use of all state agencies as well as his own. "The topography of the state is the major factor that makes air transportation economical in Idaho," he wrote, and listed uses a plane would have if purchased. Like his predecessor, Bryan pointed out that he did not have enough to carry out the responsibilities the legislature had assigned him.[11]

Bryan was succeeded by W.H. "Pete" Hill. During his two years as Director of Aeronautics, 1938-1940, federal defense spending had a dramatic impact on Idaho aviation. The Civilian Pilot Training program (CPT) helped increase the number of licensed pilots in the state by 60% from 1939 to 1940, to a total of 248, and WPA projects built and improved airports all over Idaho. The first forest fire fighters were dropped by parachute in 1940, and experimental planting of fish by plane was begun, with Lionel Dean of Twin Falls as the contractor.[12]

A.A. Bennett, old Alaska bush pilot and Idaho mountain mail and freight contractor, was appointed director for 1941 and 1942. He was succeeded briefly by Lt. Col. Leverett

Courtesy Doris Willy Crowder

Chet Moulton and Mayor James Straight salute Dr. H.A. Funk of Boise with buckets of water after his first solo flight, May 21, 1940. Moulton and Funk were members of the Boise Jaycees Flying Club at the time.

Davis. Bennett, then living in Pocatello, was again in charge until Governor Arnold Williams called Chet Moulton of Boise to his office and offered him the job. Moulton, reluctant to get into a political situation, told the governor that he was not a Democrat, and that he had reservations about accepting a political appointment. Governor Williams assured him he didn't care about his politics but only wanted the best man for the job. After conferring with *Statesman* publisher James Brown, for whom he was working at the time as a pilot, Moulton decided to accept the challenge. Brown promised to support him politically if it became necessary.[13] For the next 25 years Chet Moulton was Director of Aeronautics for the State of Idaho. Thanks to the pledge made by Arnold Williams, and the resourceful leadership of Moulton, Idaho aviation was largely de-politicized for the next quarter century. Every governor, Republican or Democrat, reappointed Moulton until February, 1971. During his years as director, Idaho's programs were recognized nationally for creative approaches to aviation problems.

In September, 1970, Chet Moulton was named "General Aviation Man of the Year" by *FLYING* magazine. He was especially praised "for organization and operation of America's first state-sponsored and financed search-and-rescue unit; legislation calling for proper marking of aerial obstructions; the airport-in-a-day program and its demonstrated resourcefulness, dedication and imagination in the use of donated equipment, volunteer workers, and available raw materials; the national lead in inauguration of airport courtesy cars and the combination residence/administration building facilities as a most important asset . . . of small or non-attended airports; a proven safe pilot program, and a prominently successful airport construction program."[14]

The citation could also have listed Moulton's leadership and support of such groups as Flying Farmers, Idaho Flying Legislators, Idaho 99s, and his organization of Idaho Air Breakfasts in all parts of the state for over 20 years. He also led international air tours to Mexico and Canada in which as many as 50 aircraft sometimes participated. Long distance flying and navigational experience was gained by about a third of Idaho's licensed pilots through this program. In 1967 Moulton was named Idaho's Outstanding State Employee.[15]

Shortly after Chet Moulton took over as director of the Aeronautics Division in the Department of Public Works, a new State Department of Aeronautics was created by the legislature.[16] In 1970 a State Aeronautics Board was established with the authority to oversee

Courtesy Idaho Department of Aeronautics

In his years as Governor, Cecil Andrus has flown into most Idaho airports. Darrell Manning is at right.

the department and to appoint a director. The law took effect on July 1, 1970.[17] That November Cecil D. Andrus was elected governor, and in April, 1971, Board Chairman Cliff Hinkley of Lewiston asked for Moulton's resignation.[18] On May 3, 1971, the board voted unanimously to hire State Senator Darrell Manning of Pocatello as director, effective June 1. Manning was a veteran pilot, operator of his own flying service, had a million mile safe flying award and was an Air Force Reserve officer then flying C124 cargo planes. He had been active in Democratic politics, serving four terms in the Idaho House of Representatives and had been minority leader for two of those.[19] Manning left in 1974 to head the Idaho Department of Transportation. He was appointed Adjutant General in 1985, in command of the Idaho National Guard. He continues in 1991 to fly jet aircraft occasionally.

In July, 1974, aeronautics was transferred to the Idaho Transportation department, and its board became merely advisory to the Idaho Transportation Board as part of a general reorganization of state agencies. Upon its recommendation, Worthie Rauscher, deputy director of the Division of Aeronautics, Montana Department of Community Affairs, was hired in 1974. The position was soon given "classified" status under the Idaho State Personnel System, hopefully removing it from partisan politics. Rauscher served until 1987. The present (1991) director is William C. Miller, appointed in early 1988.[20]

COYOTE HUNTERS XI

Hunting coyotes from the air was one of the most dangerous occupations a flier could get into. The excitement of the chase appealed to many, but a pilot with a barnstormer's skills and temperament could also make a little money at it. Lamoine Stevens of Twin Falls was more successful than most.

In March, 1938, Stevens chased coyotes all over southern Idaho. "Alone, the flier heads his three-cylinder monoplane onto the tail of a fleeing coyote, then when he gets within range of the animal, hoists his sawed-off shotgun over the edge of the ship's cockpit and lets fire." Stevens killed more than 100 animals that spring and made a small profit by selling the hides. After each kill he dropped a four-foot square parachute marker to guide his partner on the ground to the spot. Back at the airport, the two men skinned out the animals. Stevens had a special permit from the State Aeronautics Division "to carry and discharge firearms from a commercial airplane."[1]

Two coyote hunters were killed on February 2, 1940, when their plane crashed into a mountainside in a snowstorm near Arco. Verne Oliver of Nampa, pilot, and Guy Givens of Melba, hunter, had been hired by sheep ranchers to rid the neighborhood of predators. It was common practice at the time for individual ranchers or county predator control boards to hire airplane hunters to go after the coyotes in winter when the snowy background made them easy to spot in open country. A Sawtooth National Forest ranger reported that 55 coyotes had been killed in 20 hours flying time, just before the fatal accident of Oliver and Givens. It was estimated that it cost $3.25 per animal to kill them from planes compared to $8.00 each by poison, trapping or stalking them on foot.[2] In this case the cost in human life made it pretty expensive.

On April 18, 1940, another coyote killing expedition near Shoshone led to a crash for pilot Kenneth Seeds of Burley and hunter Kenneth Morris. Both were hospitalized, but Seeds was released with minor injuries. Morris suffered serious spinal injuries and partial paralysis. After all such accidents, W.H. Pete Hill, Sr., who was the State Aeronautics Director in 1940 and had issued the permit, investigated.[3]

Lamoine Stevens, veteran of several years of aerial coyote hunting, crashed his BC-65 Taylorcraft in lava beds near Shoshone in January, 1941, when the engine suddenly stopped at low altitude. Floyd Silva, Shoshone rancher, was the hunter on this occasion. Although the plane was wrecked, both men suffered only cuts and bruises.[4] Silva survived another crash less than a month later while hunting coyotes from a plane piloted by Vern Chapman of Cedar City, Utah. In this case it was probably pilot error that caused the plane to run head on into a low rocky ridge near Lake Walcott east of Minidoka.[5] In the excitement of the chase a pilot could easily try to make his low-flying plane perform maneuvers it couldn't handle. We don't know how many coyotes Silva killed on these two flights, both ending in crashes, but on the debit side were two Taylorcraft airplanes, worth several thousand dollars each. Although both were probably salvageable, it made coyote hunting expensive, to say nothing of insurance premiums.

ISHS 69-26.1

As Boise Junior College campus was developed, it covered more and more of the old airport. When Gowen Field was activated, in 1941, civilian pilot training was moved back to the college for the duration.

Webb's Flying Service in 1939 had these aircraft: A Fleet biplane, Piper J4 Cub, Ryan B1 (sister to the Spirit of St. Louis), *Piper J3 Cub, and a Taylorcraft. Webb Appel, founder of the company is third from left.*

Courtesy Doris Willy Crowder

PREPARING FOR WAR XII

1940 was a turning point in the history of Idaho aviation, as it was for the world. The war in Europe was going disastrously for America's friends. Hitler's Luftwaffe and Panzer forces had conquered Poland in the Blitzkrieg of 1939, and in the spring of 1940 had crushed France, Holland and Belgium, and had driven the British off the continent at Dunkirk. President Roosevelt abandoned any pretense of neutrality in the war by urging sale of arms to Britain to bolster that island nation's defenses against the invasion everybody was sure Hitler had to launch if he was to win. Despite strong resistance in Congress to getting America involved, in March, 1941, the Lend-Lease Act passed, primarily to aid Britain, but also China and other nations fighting the Axis powers.[1]

The federally funded Civilian Pilot Training program (CPT), started in 1939, enrolled hundreds of Idaho men and women in 1940, as individual programs were established in most Idaho colleges. President Roosevelt's announced goal of 50,000 new pilots that year,[2] and the opportunity to learn to fly at government expense, attracted many who had only dreamed of flying earlier. Many who enrolled probably never expected to be called into the military, although most of the men realized that it was a possibility. Some college women who completed the course would become flight instructors. Others became ferry pilots after America got into the war in December, 1941. Most Idaho men who completed the CPT courses went on to further military flight training and served in Army, Navy or Marines. Some older Idaho fliers who had been in Army or Navy Reserve units were called up. Dr. Lyman West of Boise, popular and active in local flying circles, was made a naval medical examiner and sent on recruiting missions in Idaho, Montana and Wyoming. He and Lt. Commander Bert Creighton signed up 22 young Boiseans in September, 1940, before flying on to Pocatello.[3] West would be killed in the crash of a Navy plane during the war.

Among the veteran pilots who gave flight instruction in the 1940 CPT programs were George Cooke, E.A. Phillips, and Johnny Vickers at The College of Idaho; Ray Crowder, Malcolm Parsons, George Perry, Lyman Choate and Jack McConnell at Boise Junior College, and Harry Clark, Ray Clark, and Allen Platt at Northwest Nazarene College.[4] Bill Woods, who taught briefly in the Nampa program, bought 120 acres northwest of Boise in 1940 and built his own field and hangars where later CPT courses were offered. Woods called his airport Floating Feather.[5] It was later his base for back country flying of all kinds.

Trainers used in the various CPT programs included Taylor and Piper Cubs, Fleet biplanes, Porterfield 65s and Ryan STAs. The latter were all-metal low-wing monoplanes, used at Webb's Flying Service for the Boise Junior College program. The University of Idaho at Moscow and U. of I. Southern Branch at Pocatello also had CPT programs in 1940. Among those who got their training at Moscow was James Trail of Eagle, later a Brigadier General and Commander of the Idaho Air National Guard. His flight instructor at the University was Frank Wiley, a Montanan who would later write an aviation history of his state, *Montana and the Sky*.[6]

In addition to the hundreds in Idaho who learned to fly in federal programs there were others who paid for private instruction in flying schools just because it was an attractive and exciting recreation. Young women who did not

Courtesy Margaret Pinneo Tillotson

Webb's Flying Service flight instructors pose for a night picture in front of their Ryan STA trainers, as their lady friends look on. Left to right: Eddie Dunne, Jack McConnell, Malcolm Parsons, Ray Crowder and Val Berriochoa.

Courtesy Doris Willy Crowder

Webb's fleet of Ryan STAs and flight instructors lined up at the new airport, 1940.

qualify for government approved courses usually joined clubs and learned to fly together. Jaycee flying clubs in Boise and Nampa, for example, sponsored instruction and bought planes that were shared by members. Webb's Flying Service in Boise trained many others to fly, even though they were contractors for the Junior College CPT program.[7]

Boise Valley Flying Service, Allen K. Platt instructor and manager, also offered lessons. In two ads in the *Statesman* on May 5, 1940, Platt offered a variety of services: "If you are interested in an airplane ride, a charter trip, instruction, or if you are interested in buying a new ship, get in touch with Allen at the Boise Airport . . . our low prices will surprise you." Platt was local dealer for Piper Cubs, Coupes and Cruisers. He also was instructor for the Boise Jaycees Flying Club. Allen Platt, who began flying in 1930 and had flown five years in the U.S. Navy,[8] was killed after the war while flying a helicopter rescue mission in the mountains.[9]

When unlimited expansion of the Army Air Corps was authorized by Congress on May 24, 1940, Harry W. Morrison reminded officials "We have available here in Boise not only the largest airport in the state, but one of the best located and largest fields in the entire West." Boise's inland location was cited as another advantage, in line with President Roosevelt's plan presented to Congress."[10]

Meanwhile, even before the 1941 approval of Lend-Lease, plans were being made for flights of American planes over Idaho on their way to Britain via Canada. In June, 1940, Idaho Falls was rumored to be under consideration as a refueling stop for 600 fighters en route from North American Aviation in California to a Canadian field.[11] After Lend-Lease was approved by Congress in March, 1941, hundreds of planes routinely landed at Idaho ports on their way to Canada. Lockheed Hudson bombers could be seen in Boise, painted with blue circle and red dot R.A.F. roundels.

Among young Idahoans who could not wait to fight the Nazis was Virgil Olson of Boise. He received a commission in the R.A.F. in July, 1940, after serving earlier on the continent with British land forces and escaping at Dunkirk. His mother told the *Statesman,* "When Lindbergh was here Virgil was thrilled to his toes with the great aviator. Why I could hardly get the boy home for dinner, he was so determined to stay down at the field and see the Lone Eagle and the *Spirit of St. Louis.*" Olson had served a hitch in the U.S. Navy before going to England to join the fight against Hitler.[12]

After receiving word that Boise had been chosen as the site of a major Air Corps bombardment and service base, city officials and the Chamber of Commerce began raising the $35,000 expected to be needed as a match for federal funds. Mayor James Straight announced that Boise's air base would be headquarters for at least 54 twin-engine medium bombers, home field for about 260 officers and 1,600 enlisted men, and that a service unit would have 40 officers and 700 enlisted men.[13] Although CPT programs had been moved away from many of the country's larger airports, Boise Junior College was assured that it could continue to use the new airport for several months yet.[14]

Credit for bringing a major air base to Boise was generally given to Idaho Adjutant General M.G. McConnel, Mayor Straight, Chamber aviation chairman H. Westerman Whillock, Harry Morrison, Frank Hummel, Leo J. Falk, Walter York, Ernest Day, J. Lynn Driscoll and Robert Overstreet, but others also worked quietly and effectively in support of first, building the new field, and second, securing the base.[15]

Even before construction got under way on the new Army air base,Boise continued to receive approval of WPA projects for airport improvements previously requested. On October 12 Senator D. Worth Clark announced that Boise would get $46,670 for construction of new runways and an apron in front of United Air Lines' hangar. A mid-month summary revealed that the WPA already had constructed 18,360 feet of runways, 1,624 feet of taxi strips, and 46,000 square yards of turning circles at the new Boise field. The administration building attached to United's hangar was also funded in large part by the WPA.[16]

On Tuesday, November 12, 1940, the City Council formally adopted the name "Boise Air

Courtesy Boise City Archives

Gowen Field's giant steel hangar was built in a hurry in 1941 to accommodate B17 bombers. The traffic control tower at right went up at the same time.

Courtesy Boise City Archives

Aprons and runways were rushed to completion as Gowen Field Army Air Base took shape in 1941.

Terminal" for the facility, on recommendation of the Chamber of Commerce aviation committee.[17] The name has continued in use ever since.

In January, 1941, two Boise construction companies received the contract to build what was to be known as Gowen Field. The city leased its airport to the U.S. Army for the duration of the war, and work began on the largest single construction job in Boise history to that time. Morrison-Knudsen and J.O. Jordan & Son were the successful bidders after merging interests for the job. One hundred twenty barracks buildings, mess halls, a hospital, recreation center, theater, and administration buildings were included in the $1,250,000 project. To be bid separately were a housing project and $250,000 worth of field improvement. J.O. Jordan, in charge of building the barracks in the first phase, was successful bidder for the housing project at $325,300. They were to construct 100 four- to five-room houses near the airport for Army families.[18] The war America was not yet in was already beginning to affect drastically families, towns and cities all over Idaho, nearly a year before Pearl Harbor.

On January 15, 1941, the first Air Corps units were organized for assignment to Boise when facilities were ready for them. The 42nd Bombardment Group, 20th Wing, commanded by Major John Hart, and the 16th Reconnaissance Squadron, under Captain David Motherwell, were to be formed from veterans in other units and recruits. The 39th Air Base Group was also formed that month for assignment to Boise.[19] In anticipation of this enormous boost to the population of the Boise area by mid-summer, Mayor Straight urged citizens to plan recreational activities for the 2,600 service men then expected. "We will want to take these boys into our hearts and should 'make room' now for them," said the Mayor. "Our families going on weekend mountain trips will want to take one or two Air Corps boys with them. Boys from the East and South will be especially appreciative. Caravans to scenic points will be popular. Dances, softball, baseball, band concerts, tennis tournaments, swimming meets, lodge attendance, extra church services, home entertainment and downtown recreation rooms must all be planned ahead."[20]

The local effort Mayor Straight outlined in January, 1941, was essentially what the U.S.O. (United Service Organizations) would be created to provide on a national scale in June, 1941. First formed as United Service Organizations for National Defense, the U.S.O. was a partnership of Y.M.C.A., Y.W.C.A., National Catholic Community Service, Jewish Welfare Board, Salvation Army and National Travelers Aid Association. A contract with the federal government provided that U.S.O. would raise $10,765,000 in the first year, and that the U.S. would build necessary facilities. Before 1941 was over more than $16 million had been contributed by the private sector.[21]

Actual construction of the Boise base began on January 21, 1941. Well drillers, road crews, carpenters, surveyors, telephone linemen and laborers swarmed over the site. Excavation for the foundation of the first of 120 buildings was started. A fence was put up and guards were posted. Morrison-Knudsen Co. moved equipment to the site of a new four mile long railway spur to be built as fast as possible. It was needed to bring in lumber, cement, and other construction materials. On January 29, final approval of all plans was received from the U.S. Army Corps of Engineers in Portland, and contractors were told they had 90 days to complete the work. Calls for bids went out on a variety of materials, including 737 rolls of waterproof sheathing paper and 1,008 kegs of nails. Boise-Payette Lumber Co. had already contracted to supply most of the lumber and carload lots were ready for delivery as soon as the railway spur was completed. Until then lumber was being trucked to the site.[22]

On February 4, 1941, Lt. Col. Lowell H. Smith, Commander of the 39th Air Base Group at Fort Douglas, Utah, flew into Boise in a B17 Flying Fortress, reportedly to be commander of the new station. He recalled that he had been one of the World War I pilots who came to Boise's polo grounds in 1919 with Major Carl Spaatz's Victory Loan flying circus.[23] Smith was internationally famous as the leader of the first round-the-world flight in 1924. Four Dou-

Courtesy Eugene F. Miller

The 303rd Bomb Group in formation flying exercise over Boise, May, 1942. The Flying Fortresses became a familiar sight to people in southern Idaho.

Courtesy Idaho Air National Guard

B17 Flying Fortresses lined up inspection, Gowen Field.

glas seaplanes, named *Chicago, New Orleans, Boston* and *Seattle,* took off from Lake Washington in Seattle on April 26, 1924, headed northwesterly on a northern hemisphere route that would take them more than 26,000 miles. *Seattle* and *Boston* were wrecked along the way, leaving only two planes to finish the flight. Lt. Smith was warmly welcomed in Paris on Bastille Day, July 14, 1924, touched North American soil again on August 31 at Labrador, and shook hands with President Calvin Coolidge in Washington, D.C., on September 8. When the fliers reached journey's end in Seattle, 50,000 people turned out to greet them.[24]

By mid-March, 1941, activity at the air base was feverish. Building permits had reached $2 million and were expected to continue to grow. The more than 1,000 men working on the project came from all over the state. Officials said 40 communities were represented on a monthly payroll that averaged $200 per man. Skilled carpenters got $250.[25]

On March 12 the Air Corps said that the new base commander would be Lt. Col. Robin A. Day, not famous flier Lowell Smith as announced earlier. The military was obviously shuffling personnel fast with all of the new responsibilities it was assuming overnight. Lt. Col. Day arrived from McChord Field, outside Tacoma, on March 12, and set up an office in the municipal air terminal, pending completion of his own headquarters building on the south side of the field.[26]

On March 19, 1941, the first contingent of 22 Boeing Flying Fortresses with British insignia landed in Boise as part of a Lend-Lease shipment to Britain. Although flown by Army Air Corps pilots from McChord Field, the big bombers carried officials of the British Embassy in Washington, D.C., and members of the British Air Mission. All stayed at the Owyhee Hotel overnight, and when weather was bad next day, decided to delay departure since none of the pilots had flown over the Rocky Mountains before. The British politely submitted to interviews by the local press, but were noncommittal on military subjects. They did insist that Britain would win the war, especially now that American aid was forthcoming.[27]

On March 23, 1941, H. Westerman Whillock, candidate for Mayor, predicted that following the war commercial aviation would do for Boise what railroading did for Omaha. "America will have vast surpluses of planes and trained aviation personnel when world peace is restored," he said. "I believe that we then shall see the greatest chapter in the development of commercial aviation . . . Boise will profit immensely because it is ideally suited to commercial flying."[28] Whillock, who would be elected, had been an active supporter of local aviation ever since he arrived in 1934 from Medford, Oregon. He purchased half interest in a World War I Curtiss Jenny owned by Dr. Lyman West, and learned to fly with Weber Appel. He, like Dr. West, was a Naval Reserve officer and was called to active service during the war, but not as a flier. Upon resuming his mayoral duties after the war, Whillock appointed the first airport commission and continued to be a leader in projects to help local aviation. He later owned and operated radio station KBOI and Channel 2 Television.[29]

On St. Patrick's Day, 1941, the first North American B-25 bomber appeared in Boise, one of three being flown from McChord Field, Washington, to Wright Field, in Dayton, Ohio. The reporter who described its appearance called it "freakish" because of its tricycle landing gear, but said it was "ultra modern," top secret, and heavily guarded. Crew members refused to comment on its speed or other vital statistics.[30]

The first full company of soldiers to arrive at Boise's air base was the 253rd Quartermaster Company from Fort Douglas, Utah. They came by truck convoy in April, 1941, and were soon telling everybody how much they liked the city — especially the girls. The men, mostly from Arkansas and Missouri, were proud of their baseball and basketball teams, and of a newspaper they published every two weeks. When publication resumed at the new station the Quartermaster men called it *The Boise Bugle*.[31]

In July, 1941, the Boise air base was officially named Gowen Field in honor of Lt. Paul Gowen of Caldwell, killed in line of duty while flying a twin-engine B-10 bomber in Panama, July 11, 1938. Gowen was an honor graduate of West Point. A brother, William Gowen of Boise, was a well known local pilot who had flown the Idaho back country since 1931.[32]

The mission assigned to Gowen Field was to train bomber crews, first with Boeing B17 Flying Fortresses and later with Consolidated B24 Liberators. Both planes were long-range four-engine heavy bombers, armed with gun turrets. The first B17s arrived in 1941, not long after the base was activated. Units assigned were Headquarters and Headquarters Squadron, 42nd Bombardment Group; 75th, 76th and 77th Bombardment Squadrons, and 16th Reconnaissance Squadron.[33] Boeing had been turning out its B17 model Ds for several months before the Japanese attack on Pearl Harbor, December 7, 1941, brought America into the war, and Gowen Field had a head start in training crews for the plane that would be the backbone of the American bomber force in Europe. In 1941 only 42 B17 Ds were built, but later models, with improved armament, numbered over 10,000 before the war was over.[34]

Courtesy Eugene F. Miller

Top and right: On line for inspection, Gowen Field, April 11, 1942. Boeing B17s.

THE WAR YEARS XIII

"Gowen Field on Full War Basis" read an *Idaho Statesman* headline on December 8, 1941. "Civilian, police, and military groups in Boise and southwest Idaho moved swiftly into defense lines Sunday as the nation prepared for sabotage and fifth-column activity following the sudden Japanese attack on Hawaii. Gowen Field enlisted men and officers were quickly recalled to their base."[1]

Getting them there was no simple matter on a Sunday afternoon, with about a thousand men in town on pass. Roads to the base were jammed with cars and trucks taking them back, with motorcycle police escorts. Hundreds more gathered at the Boise police station waiting for transportation. "Bombing planes from the field, flying over the city, lent a realistic atmosphere to the day's activities," said the *Statesman.*[1]

Guards were posted at dams and power plants, although Idaho Power Company officials said they didn't think armed guards would be necessary. Visits to the company's facilities had already been restricted for some time.

The Civil Aeronautics Authority grounded all private planes and temporarily canceled all private pilot licenses. Amateur radio operations were prohibited.[3] The immediate fear of sabotage was due to the memory of the use of covert activities in the Spanish Civil War of 1936-39, when the term "fifth column" first came into use, and because of Germany's successful employment of terrorist tactics in the defeat of France and the Low Countries. Movies, books and newspaper stories had made Americans sharply aware of threats from within by enemy agents or sympathizers.

Japan's attack on Pearl Harbor made many people fearful that Idaho's small Japanese-American population might become fifth columnists, but there was none of the hysteria that was experienced in some Pacific Coast areas. Probably acting on Federal Bureau of Investigation directives, within hours of the attack Governor Chase Clark issued an executive order that all Japanese nationals were to remain in their homes until their status was determined. Most local officials were unaware that Boise Valley even had any Japanese nationals, although communities of second generation Japanese-Americans, and a few older Japanese who had been here for more than 30 years were prominent farmers around Nampa, Caldwell and Emmett. The day after Governor Clark's order a delegation from the Japanese-American Citizen's League called on him with assurances that they were "100 percent Americans" and pledged their "wholehearted assistance to our government, state and communities."[4]

By coincidence, on the day the news of Pearl Harbor came, Brig. Gen. William E. Hershey, national director of selective service, was on a train coming to Boise. On arrival he said, "The United States can be tougher'n hell if the people get mad enough." He was in Boise for a meeting with state officials on the draft, and headed back for Washington next day. He told reporters that the nation's resources were "endless," with 41 million men between the ages of 16 to 64, and that war production could be speeded up as much as needed.[5]

Col. Charles B. Oldfield, Gowen Field commander, talked to the press on December 8 and laid out rules governing news of the base now that war had started: Absolute secrecy would be maintained on the movement of troops and planes "for the defense and security of the United States." He said that Gowen Field's mission was primarily to train and service tactical units, but that could change. Groups and organizations stationed at the base could no longer be mentioned by name or number, as publication of such information could help the enemy. Security measures were increased against sabotage, attack, or espionage, and armed guards patrolled all perimeters. No automobiles could be parked near fences. Airplanes other than military would fly over the field at their own risk, and would be treated "as enemy aircraft."[6]

Training of bomber crews was intensified in the months after Pearl Harbor, and news of crashes of planes on training flights began to appear with regularity in the papers. The Air Corps could hardly keep them secret, since they often happened where people saw them. By mid-January, 1942, names of casualties were being released to the press. On January 26, 1942, a Boise Valley unit of the Civil Air Patrol was organized with Eddie Dunn as executive officer. The CAP would be involved in many search missions for downed Gowen Field planes and personnel in the months ahead.[7]

By January, 1942, a Boise man was already in England as a volunteer in the Royal Air Force's American Eagle squadron. A Boise mother was thrilled to hear the voice of her son, Sgt.-Pilot Jerry Doherty, on local radio January 31 broadcasting from London.[8] Duane Beeson, another Boisean, had gone to Canada to join the Royal Canadian Air Force in 1941. He arrived in England on March 29, 1942. Beeson would become one of the top American aces in the European Theater, flying Spitfires and Hurricanes, then P47s and P51s after transfer into the American 8th Air Force. He was credited with 19.33 victories.[9] Another Boisean, Ross E. Rowell, a pioneer U.S. Marine Corps flier who had won the Distinguished Flying Cross for bombing missions in Nicaragua in 1928,[10] was promoted to Major General that month.

Eleanor Roosevelt, who became the first U.S. president's wife to fly in June, 1933, was in Boise briefly on March 5, 1942. Reporters learned of her arrival but were not allowed an interview since she was asleep aboard the plane.

Training flight crashes continued to make the news in 1942. On March 17 four men were killed when their bomber went down three miles south of Gowen field. On March 31, William M. Skinner, Jr., who had learned to fly in the CPT program conducted by Webb's Flying Service for Boise Junior College, and had later earned his instructor's rating, was killed while flying with a student pilot. On March 5, 1942, another Gowen bomber went down at Bridge, in Cassia County south of Malta, killing all eight crewmen. The crew of a bomber with engine trouble over Buhl was luckier, when all six men parachuted safely. On September 21, 1942, another bomber crashed and burned at Gowen Field killing three. Three others later died of injuries. Five soldiers who pulled men from the burning wreckage were later given medals for heroism.

Col. Eddie Rickenbacker, America's top ace in World War I, visited Gowen Field on March 31, and in a speech in Boise blasted war profiteering. Captain Hewett T. Wheless, an air hero of the Philippine battle, praised by President Roosevelt in a nationwide broadcast, was assigned to Gowen Field in April, 1942. Maj. Gen. F.L. Martin, Commander of the Second Air Force inspected Gowen Field on April 22 and called it "one of the best." In July the installation was named a "home base" for the training of Flying Fortress pilots, and on August 16, 1942, Second Air Force headquarters designated it a "model base."

The *Gowen Field Beacon,* a semi-monthly newspaper, released its first issue on September 2, 1942. Other amenities for airmen at the base were visits by radio and movie celebrities. Pinky Tomlin, radio star, performed on September 19, and actor Andy Devine appeared October 20. G.I.s who went into town for entertainment had a chance to hear Sir Thomas Beecham conduct the Seattle Symphony, listen to opera star Rise Stevens, or dance to the bands of Tommy Dorsey or Ted Fio Rito. Daley Brothers Circus was also in town that summer. A number of night clubs opened in Boise, especially to attract Gowen soldiers; they proved hard for the city and the M.P.s to control. Both the base command and city officials were worried about teenage girls and too much liquor in

Courtesy Eugene F. Miller

Courtesy Eugene F. Miller

Top: 303rd Bomb Group in close formation over the Mountain Home Desert, May 8, 1942. Victory in Europe was three years away to the day, and some of these planes and their crews would pay the price to bring it about.

Above: General Martin inspecting the 303rd Bomb Group, Gowen Field, May, 1942.

the clubs.

On April 27, 1942, Pocatello received word that an air base similar to Gowen Field had been approved by the War Department. An area of 3,500 acres was acquired and the field was built and manned before the year was over. Gen. Leo J. Leeburn was first commander of the base. It flew B17s, B26s, P47s and B34s before being closed down in 1945. Like other wartime aviation facilities, it had its share of training fatalities and accidents.[12]

The Army began site studies for a new air base at Mountain Home on November 13, 1942, and by Christmas ground had been broken. The population of the little desert town grew rapidly. The choice of a site a few miles to the south was prompted by its wide open surroundings, by the fact that a short railroad spur from the Union Pacific mainline would facilitate supply, and because of generally good flying weather year-round. The availability of many square miles of virtually uninhabited country in three directions was an asset for training missions. In early February, 1943, members of the Idaho legislature were given a tour of the new base as guests of J.A. Terteling and Sons, the construction contractors, and the Aero Club of Boise. They viewed giant earth-moving equipment used to level the field, and an extensive sub-surface drainage system being installed.[13] Mountain Home was to be the site of a B29 Super Fortress base, a plane Boeing had been developing for many years. In fact, the basic model was first flown in 1939. When America entered the war in December, 1941, 250 B29s were ordered, and even while the Mountain Home base was being built the contract was doubled.[14]

On May 20, 1942, Col. Charles B. Oldfield, base commander at Gowen Field, was transferred to Rapid City, South Dakota, and succeeded by Col. Arthur J. Melanson.[15] In January, 1943, Melanson led a tour of inspection for visiting Second Air Force brass — Brig. Gen. Nathan Forrest and Brig. Gen. Gerald Williams.[16] The high cost in planes and lives in training missions continued to rise in 1943. On January 16 a Gowen Field B17 crashed near Kuna killing all nine men aboard.[17] On January 26, the wreck of an Army Trainer, missing since December 9, was found by Civil Air Patrol ground crews near Bennett Mountain north of Mountain Home. CAP civilian pilots Waldo Thurber and Wilson Kellogg spotted the ship three days after it disappeared, but bad flying weather had delayed confirmation and deep snows had kept ground searchers away.[18] The first news that another bomber, origin unknown, had gone down near a frozen lake in mountains north of Boise appeared in the *Idaho Statesman* on February 4. Ten days later five of the crew of eight were rescued by "miracle pilot" Penn Stohr. Three others who had started to walk out from Loon Lake in deep snow were later found and rescued.[19] (See page 60.) On April 1, 1943, a bomber from Walla Walla Air Base crashed in the mountains near Challis. Wreckage was still burning when a rescue crew reached the spot, but no airmen were found. All had been able to bail out, but only five reached Middle Fork ranger station where they were able to telephone for help. Again it was Penn Stohr who landed his ski-equipment Travelair to carry the men out.[20] The others were found later.

A Flying Fortress veered out of control on takeoff from Gowen Field April 14, 1943, and struck two other planes and a shed. Five crewmen were killed and eight others hospitalized. A May 4 crash at Mountain Home killed the entire crew of another B17 when the plane exploded on impact.[21]

In mid-May, 1943, Gowen Field began to convert from B17s to B24s. The big Liberators were dubbed "stuffed whales" and "old cows" by crews used to the longer and slimmer B17s. Some wags said the fat-bellied B24s looked like "the box cars the B17s came in." A training unit from Consolidated Aircraft came to Gowen to retrain crews to handle the bigger and faster ships, which had already proven their effectiveness in Europe.[22] In June, European theater veterans who had flown some of the first B24 raids were transferred to Gowen Field.

By the end of July Mountain Home Air Base was nearly complete. J.A. Terteling & Sons of Boise, the contractors, were awarded the war department's "E" award for efficiency in its construction.

The first contingent of WACs arrived at Gowen on May 9, 1943, with auxiliary status. They were inducted into the regular army on August 24. A "WAC Salute Day" was held at the field on December 12.

Governor Bottolfsen called a meeting of Idaho aviators and "aviation boosters" to form an aircraft pool for transportation emergencies that might arise during the winter months. All private planes had been moved away from Boise Air Terminal/Gowen Field at the beginning of the war, and civilian flying was greatly curtailed. Pilots welcomed the chance to be of service, and 30 planes were enrolled.

Losses of bombers and lives were heavy in 1943 Idaho military operations. Thirteen planes crashed, and 55 crew members died. The worst disaster was at Mountain Home on October 24 when a mid-air collision killed all 16 aboard the two bombers. Happily another 28 airmen survived with minor injuries, some by parachuting.

The visiting celebrity who attracted the most attention at Gowen Field in 1943 was the movie star, Lt. Jimmy Stewart. He arrived for duty as a flight training officer on Valentine's Day, appropriately enough, for many young Boise women were eager to see the boyish and likeable actor.[23] One local girl who dated him remembers that he got well acquainted with the managers of local movie theaters — the *Ada* (originally, and now, the *Egyptian*), the *Boise,* the *Granada* and the *Pinney.* He was especially fond of the organ in the *Ada* and would come down after hours to hear Nevin McCord, manager for Menmar Theaters, play. Stewart, who could play the piano, got Nevin to show him how to use the many special effects on the theater organ. Jimmy's favorite tunes, or at least the ones he played from memory, were *Up A Lazy River* and *Ragtime Cowboy Joe.* He was often a guest at the Aero Club, and liked to dance at the TK Club on Broadway Avenue. When he left Gowen Field in August, 1943 he had been promoted to Captain. Boise friends gave him a farewell party.[24]

Courtesy Malcolm Parsons Estate

In May, 1943, Gowen Field's B17s were replaced with Consolidated B24 Liberators. This aerial view shows the bigger B24s lined up at left.

With the war going well on all fronts, security measures at Gowen Field were somewhat relaxed in 1944. In March a midnight curfew for all personnel was lifted. Open houses for the public attracted 3,000 civilians in August and another 2,000 in September. Training of B24 crews continued to be costly, however. Seven planes crashed that year with the loss of 45 crew members.[25]

The European war ended on May 8, 1945. A Boeing B29 Superfortress was displayed at Gowen Field on August 1, and thousands went to see it. Less than a week later the B29 *Enola Gay* would drop the first atomic bomb on Hiroshima, followed by the Japanese surrender on August 14. Before the war ended, nine more bombers on training flights from Idaho bases crashed in 1945, killing 37 crewmen. In March, three planes went down in one week.[26]

The war years saw United Air Lines continue to provide regular mail and passenger service to Boise on its Portland to Salt Lake City line. United was allowed to continue use of its pre-war facilities at Boise Air Terminal, even though all other non-military aviation had been moved away from the Gowen Field bomber training operation.

ISHS 65-45.17

It was a great day for Bert Zimmerly when he could sign a contract for $465,000 worth of new passenger planes for his young airline, August 13, 1946. Wellwood E. Beall of Boeing Aircraft Company looked on.

The most successful intra-state airline to that time got its start on April 10, 1944, when Bert Zimmerly of Lewiston made the first of a series of test flights to Boise. He had earlier filed an application with the Civil Aeronautics Board to establish an ambitious 16 city network that would cover the northwest. Zimmerly Air Transport had been formed to do trial runs between Idaho cities by visionary aviation men who saw the possibilities and need for air service among a number of Idaho and northwest towns then without it. In 1944 there was no air line operating between north and south Idaho, and southern Idaho towns had no scheduled service to Boise where connection with United could be made.[27] Bert Zimmerly and Tom Croson of Lewiston, who had been primarily involved in training pilots, and Gwin Hicks of Coeur d'Alene, General Manager of Buroker-Hicks Flying Service, had met in Kansas City in 1943 to discuss the formation of an airline.[28]

The first step, if CAB permission was to be granted for an interstate "feeder line," was to prove the need for such service, and the capability of the operator to provide it. The name Empire Airlines had been chosen before any test flights were made, and the application to CAB was made in that name well before incorporation in October, 1944.[29]

Flying a Cessna Airmaster with three passengers aboard, Bert Zimmerly came from Lewiston to Boise April 10 to begin to test public reception of the proposed line. He did not need CAB permission to fly passengers in Idaho, and felt he could take a long step toward a more ambitious interstate feeder network if he proved first that Idaho towns needed and wanted it. The warm welcome Zimmerly received in Boise on April 10 was heartening, and would turn out to be typical of his visits to other towns. Governor C.A. Bottolfsen personally greeted him at the college field, along with Harry Morrison, president of Morrison-Knudsen Corporation, and Lt. Col. Leverett Davis, director of The Civil Air Patrol.

At a luncheon in Hotel Boise Governor Bottolfsen said, "Today's meeting is the first step toward expanded air service in Idaho and I am happy to have a part in welcoming Mr. Zimmerly to Boise. In this state of magnificent distances, we need improvement and expansion of all types of transportation, but particularly in air service." Col. Davis, CAP chief, said Zimmerly was the best qualified operator in Idaho to inaugurate such an air line, citing the fact that he had had a commercial pilot's certificate since 1935, had logged over 5,000 hours flying time, and was familiar with most of the routes his planes would travel.[30]

ISHS 65-45.11

Zimmerly Airlines all metal Boeing 247 flying over Idaho mountains. The planes carried 10 passengers, a flight attendant, a pilot and co-pilot.

On Monday, June 12, 1944, Zimmerly Air Transport began regular daily service between Lewiston and Boise on a 30-day trial basis, using four-passenger Cessnas and a six-passenger Travelair 6000. A crew of seven pilots was hired to make the daily flights, scheduled to take two hours between Boise and Lewiston. Under ideal conditions it was often made in 90 minutes. The fare was $15.00 one way and $27.00 round trip. In July, service was extended to Twin Falls, Pocatello, Idaho Falls and Coeur d'Alene. Bert Zimmerly appreciated the power of advertising. He not only took ads in local newspapers of the towns he visited, but usually invited a reporter to take the inaugural flight. The result was a lot of favorable publicity. The *Lewiston Morning Tribune,* following closely a home-grown enterprise, gave a daily report of how many people had flown in and out of the city's new "million dollar airport," and often listed their names. Business was so good (and the planes so small) that Zimmerly soon had a two month backlog of reservations. He put on extra flights for special events, and in July, 1943, bought three 10-passenger Boeing 247s. Larger lines like United were phasing out the Boeings in favor of 21-passenger Douglas DC3s at this time.

George Cooke, Chief pilot for Empire Airlines, and later for West Coast, receives an award from Oregon's head of Aeronautics while Chet Moulton, Idaho Aeronautics director looks on.

After a CAB hearing in San Francisco in November, 1944, and a final one in Washington, D.C., in October, 1945, Empire Airlines was certified and granted permission to operate for three years, beginning May 22, 1946. Recertification would then be considered. The routes granted inside Idaho were between Idaho Falls and Boise, with intermediate stops at Pocatello, Burley, Twin Falls and Gooding; interstate, Empire would fly from Boise to Spokane, with stops at Payette, Idaho, Ontario, Baker, LaGrande and Pendleton, Oregon, and Walla Walla, Washington, Lewiston, Clarkston, Moscow-Pullman, and Coeur d'Alene. The war was over and most of Idaho's larger cities now had regularly scheduled air passenger service.[31] A number of them would lose it in the postwar years.

Courtesy Gwin Hicks

Dynamic Gwin Hicks, left, was considered by many the most effective airline public relations man of his day.

ISHS 65-45.31

Empire Airlines pilots in about 1947. Chief Pilot George Cooke is at top right.

ISHS 65-45.15

Historic arrival of Zimmerly Airline's first Boeing 247D in Boise, 1943. The plane, a giant for its day, fits easily into United's drive-through hangar.

Courtesy BLM/BIFC

Smoke jumper coming down.

FLYING FIRE FIGHTERS XIV

A fire fighting crew first parachuted into Idaho's mountains on July 12, 1940. Dick Johnson, of Johnson Flying Service, Missoula, Montana, was the pilot. The plane was a Travelair. Rufus Robinson and Earl Cooley were the men who made the leap that began a new era in the history of fighting forest fires.[1]

Training of that first crew began in October, 1939, at Winthrop, Washington, in Okanogan National Forest — experimental at first, because nobody yet knew if men could land safely in rugged, forested, mountain terrain. Equipment was tested by professionals from the Eagle Parachute Co. under a variety of conditions before the first Forest Service employees were allowed to try. Each man was outfitted with a 30-foot parachute in a back pack, a 27-foot emergency chute in a chest pack, a football helmet and wire mesh face mask, a padded jump suit and heavy logging boots. They had ankle and back braces. Tools, rations, and other equipment were dropped separately.[2]

After 10 training jumps the men were considered ready for the real test. A small fire on Martin Creek in Nez Perce National Forest provided the target for the jump made by Robinson and Cooley on July 12. As Earl Cooley says, in his fine reminiscence *Trimotor and Trail,* the whole program might have been called off if either he or Robinson had not survived that first jump. As it was, Cooley had trouble with his chute and barely made it, Robinson was carried far beyond the target, and Merle Lundigan, the cargo dropper, nearly fell out of the plane without a chute. Happily, that first drop into what is now the Selway-Bitterroot Wilderness did not end in tragedy.[3]

There would be tragedies in the years ahead, however, like the Mann Gulch fire in Helena National Forest in August, 1949, in which 13 young firefighters died. Earl Cooley dedicated his book to their memory.

Planes had been used for parachuting supplies to fire fighters for several years, but 1940 was the first year that men were dropped. Water bombing from planes had been tried since the 1920s, but had never been very effective due to the small amount of water the planes of those days could lift, to say nothing of the difficulty of hitting the target. On any large fire water bombing had been nearly useless.[4] The summer of 1940 was a bad one for lightning-caused fires in both Idaho and Montana. On July 15, just three days after the smoke jumpers made their first drop, a plane parachuting supplies to fire crews went down in the Bitterroot Mountains killing pilot Robert Maracich, and seriously injuring Deel Clabaugh. Earl Vance, a Missoula pilot, took two Forest Service parachutists with him to look for the plane and to drop them with first aid supplies if possible. They could not make that jump, but others were made later that summer.[5]

The Army had been interested in the training given to smoke jumpers from the beginning, and in August, 1940, Lt. Robert H. Rankin, in a feature story in the *Idaho Statesman,* explained that interest: "Since the use of parachute troops by Germany in the present war, it is evident that the use of such combat units will become an important function of all modern armies. The United States has recognized the importance of this new method of investing enemy territory and steps have been taken to train our own parachute troops. Be this as it may, the United States Forest Service has long been thinking of the possibility of parachuting fire fighters to areas which could not be other-

Courtesy BLM/BIFC

Courtesy BLM/BIFC

Top right: Boise Interagency Fire Center as it looked in the early 1980s. It has grown a lot since.

Top: Modular Airborne Fire Fighting System in action, laying a load of chemical retardant.

Left: Boeing B17 Flying Fortresses were stripped of all armament and modified internally to carry large loads of retardant.

Courtesy BLM/BIFC

wise reached. Working quite independently of other agencies, the Forest Service has successfully demonstrated the idea and 'smoke jumpers' are likely to comprise the newest addition to the forest fire control forces of this country."

Rankin's use of the term "smoke jumper" was one of the earliest to appear in print. He explained the advantage of parachuting fire fighters over sending them in on foot: "Large crews traveling over rough country often spend much of their energy in travel before they reach the flames, and so are too exhausted to do immediate effective work." Since crews had been supplied by air with food and equipment since 1937, using burlap parachutes, Rankin explained, "the parachuting of the fire fighters themselves was the next logical step in forest fire control by air." The availability of small portable radios in 1940 was a significant communications factor in making aerial drops practicable. The radios used at that time weighed six pounds each and were "not quite so large as a loaf of sandwich bread."

Photos accompanying Rankin's article show that Johnson Flying Service Ford Trimotors were used — a ship that would, because of its size, power, and lift, be the workhorse of aerial fire fighting for many years.

Nick Mamer, flying out of Spokane, was a pioneer in supplying fire crews from the air as well as spotting fires. He and Forest Inspector Howard Flint are credited with being "The inspiration of many of the subsequent uses of aircraft, particularly in the Northern Rocky Mountains."[7] They had dropped kegs of water from a Ford Trimotor as early as 1929, but serious development of techniques for dropping water and chemical retardants did not come until the 1950s. By that time, large numbers of surplus military aircraft were available, with sufficient size and power to carry enough water or chemicals to be effective. Most models of World War II bombers were adapted to this service, from Navy TBM torpedo bomb-

Courtesy BLM/BIFC

Helicopters of all sizes have been used for delivering water to fires, using scoop buckets like these.

It has been many years since flights of B17s have flown in formations like this on the way to a forest fire.

Courtesy BLM/BIFC

ers to B25s, B26s, B18s, and B17s. Obsolete civilian airliners also became available: DC4, DC6, and DC7, to name only a few.[8]

Smaller planes have proven to be effective for water and chemical bombing, especially those designed for crop dusting. Because of their slow speed and maneuverability these planes can land closer to a fire in small unimproved spaces, take on and dump retardant quickly and return for reloading repeatedly with a minimum of lost time. Large planes have a much larger capacity but require long paved runways, usually far from the fire.[9]

Helicopters have been used extensively in aerial fire fighting since World War II, with a great deal of experimentation with different kinds of machines and techniques. At first rotary wing aircraft were used almost exclusively for reconnaissance, but as larger military types became available, could be used to deliver firefighters, supplies, and retardant. This, over the long run, has proven to be very costly, since nearly all helicopters are operated under contract with private companies. By 1985 a Bell 214 medium helicopter rented for $3600 per hour. Despite this, large numbers of helicopters are used each fire season in Idaho because of their special fire control capabilities and the value of the resources they are able to protect.[10]

In Idaho, helicopters have proven effective for rescue of firefighters from difficult situations, and for water bombing using buckets. The chopper hovers over a river or lake, scoops up a large bucket of water, flies to the fire, dumps the load with a release mechanism, and returns for another.

Because forest and range fires are unpredictable, contingencies must always be planned for. The Modular Airborne Fire Fighting System (MAFFS) is an example. In the early 1970s Congress authorized development of a 3000 gallon pressurized tank system that could fit into a C130 military airplane without structural modifications. Tactical Air Groups in four loca-

Bucket-equipped helicopters are shown in these two dramatic views of Idaho forest fires of the 1980s.

Courtesy BLM/BIFC

tions nationally are trained annually to assure readiness for fire emergencies involving "imminent danger" to life and property, but only after all other resources are exhausted. The MAFFS can lay down a line of water or retardant about half a mile long by 60 feet wide. The annual training session was based in Boise in May, 1991, hosted by the 153rd Tactical Air Group from Cheyenne, Wyoming.[11]

Boise Interagency Fire Center is the national logistical support center for wildfire suppression. It began in 1965 as Great Basin Fire Center in temporary Idaho Army National Guard quarters at Gowen Field, after the national heads of the Bureau of Land Management and the Forest Service signed a Western Fire Coordinating Agreement. Boise was chosen as the site of the operation because of its strategic location. Construction of facilities began in 1968 after a land exchange between BLM and the State of Idaho made a site available next to Boise Air Terminal. Dedication of the first phase of building at BIFC took place in 1970. Smoke jumpers from Idaho City were moved to the center that year, and a smoke jumper training area and air tanker base were completed in 1971.

Other agencies to join BIFC were the National Weather Service, 1969, National Park Service, 1974, Bureau of Indian Affairs, 1977, and U.S. Fish and Wildlife Service, 1979. In 1976 the Center became the coordinator for logistical support in suppression of wildfires nation-wide and internationally, after an agreement with Canada for mutual support was signed that year. Aviation has played a major role in the work of the Center, as it has coordinated fire fighting from Maine to California and Canada to Mexico. BIFC's training courses in fire suppression have been accepted internationally.[12]

Courtesy BLM/BIFC

Courtesy BLM/BIFC

Top: Crop duster biplanes dump either water or retardant on range or forest wildfires. Above: Modern smoke jumpers use ram-air chutes with a drogue trailer for better control of landings.

ISHS

Above: Empire's publicity department combined several appeals in this 1960s photo: safety, sex, and glamour. Right: Empire flew Idaho teachers free as part of an Air Age Education program.

ISHS

BIGGER AND FASTER XV

When the war ended in August, 1945, military bases around the state changed status rapidly. Gowen Field began sending soldiers to discharge centers in their home states, or mustering them out in Boise if they preferred. In mid-September, Gowen was officially made one of 145 army separation centers nationwide. Flight training stopped on September 27, but not before one more B24 crashed that month killing seven. Three parachuted to safety.

On October 3, 1945, Fourth Air Force headquarters announced the "inactivation" of Mountain Home Air Force Base. This was less final than "deactivation," in military language, and it was thought Mountain Home would become a satellite operation of Gowen Field. By October 6 Gowen separation center was discharging 500 men a day. When the AAF released a list of 90 permanent bases to be retained, Gowen Field was not among them, and on October 25 news came that the base would be inactivated. By November 30 the separation center had completed its work and the process of inactivation preliminary to deactivation, or shut down, was begun. Pocatello Air Base was the only one in Idaho the Air Force planned to retain at the end of 1945, but it too was soon deactivated.[1]

In 1946 Gowen Field, which had been leased to the Army since 1941, was returned to Boise City. H. Westerman Whillock, back from service in the Navy, resumed the position of Mayor to which he had been elected before the war. One of his first official acts was to appoint an airport commission to oversee management of an enormous piece of real estate with buildings and facilities worth millions. Architect Frank Hummel was made chairman; others appointed to that first commission were Gen. Clarence E. Boggs, who served 1946-1972; J. Roger Mendenhall, 1946-1977; Gen. Walter R. York, 1946-1981; and Lt. Col. Thomas G. Lanphier, Jr., 1946-1949.[2]

Tom Lanphier had won the Navy Cross for shooting down the plane of Admiral Isoroku Yamamoto, commander of the Japanese Imperial Fleet, and mastermind of the Pearl Harbor attack. Lanphier flew 112 combat missions in the Pacific, mostly in Lockheed P38 fighters, and was credited with 5½ victories. When the Idaho Air National Guard was formed on October 13, 1946, he was appointed commander of the 190th Fighter Squadron. In November, 1946, the squadron received the first of a fleet of 25 P51 Mustang fighters. In addition to his part-time duties with the Guard, Lanphier was Managing Editor of the *Idaho Statesman* newspaper until 1949 when he left Idaho to become special assistant to Stuart Symington, chairman of the National Security Resources Board in Washington, D.C., and later first Secretary of the Air Force.[3]

Boise City leased the Gowen Field military base to the Idaho National Guard which began the process of making part of it usable again in January, 1947. With an original enrollment of 23 officers and 44 enlisted men, Tom Lanphier's command was hardly in a position to open more than a small portion of a base manned by as many as 6,000 men during the war, but active recruiting for the 190th Fighter Squadron, 190th Utility Flight, Detachment C, 242nd Air Service Group, and the 190th Weather Station began in earnest. A variety of other World War II aircraft were assigned to the Air Guard in the first two years, including three B26 medium bombers and two C47 transports. The Air Force had thousands of surplus planes at the end of the war and they were readily available. Those that could be converted for

Courtesy Idaho Air National Guard

Top: War hero Lt. Col. Tom Lanphier buzzes the tower in a P51 Mustang – the plane with which his Idaho Air National Guard was first equipped. Above: A mustang taxis in.

commercial use were sold to a host of small operators eager to get them. Planes like the B17 could rarely be adapted to other use, and most were scrapped or temporarily "mothballed" at desert sites.

Besides regular training in gunnery and mechanics, the Air Guard flew emergency missions as called upon. These ranged over the years from transporting iron lungs during the post-war polio epidemic to reconnaissance and communication support during the Teton Dam flood disaster in 1976.

On April 1, 1951, the 190th Fighter Squadron was called to active duty in the Korean War. By then it had an enlistment of 452 officers and enlisted men. Through a series of transfers and reorganizational changes over the next few years, too complicated to follow here, the Idaho Air National Guard grew in size, competence, and reputation. Beginning in 1953, world-wide Air National Guard gunnery exercises were hosted at Gowen Field, and in November that year the Guard got its first jet aircraft — T33

trainers, followed by F86A Sabre Jets to replace the P51s (by then relabeled F51, for fighter). The F86As had been used in Korea, and again the Guard was given aircraft already on their way to obsolescence. In 1955 these planes were replaced with more advanced F94B Starfires, a ship that carried a radar man in addition to the pilot. These too were soon replaced. In June, 1956, F89B Scorpions were received, much larger and more powerful than anything the Idaho Air Guard had handled before. In 1959 the unit converted to F86D/L Sabre Jets, and in November, 1964, acquired F102A Delta Daggers — the first supersonic ships stationed in Boise. In October, 1975, a new mission was assigned and new aircraft. Now a Tactical Reconnaissance Group, the Gowen Field guardsmen were given RF4C Phantom IIs, capable of flying twice the speed of sound. Throughout the years of growth and change Idaho's Air Guard and individuals within it won prestigious national awards for all phases of their work, too numerous to mention here.[4] As this is written, F4G Wild Weasels, proven highly effective combat aircraft in the Gulf War, are being assigned to Gowen Field.[5]

When Lt. Col. Lanphier left Idaho in 1949, James M. Trail replaced him. He was made Assistant Adjutant General, Air, in 1955, a position he held until his retirement with the rank of Brigadier General in 1977. Squadron and Group commanders during Gen. Trail's

Courtesy Idaho Air National Guard

Top: World-wide Air National Guard gunnery exercises were held at Gowen Field in 1953. P51s (later designated F51s) lined up before a base still much as it was in 1945. Above: The business end of an F51.

Courtesy Idaho Air National Guard

Above and left: Idaho's Air Guard entered the jet age with these F86As in 1953.

Courtesy Idaho Air National Guard

Above and left: 1959 saw the arrival of 25 F89s. Military aircraft got bigger and faster with every war and threat of war.

Courtesy Idaho Air National Guard

The needle-nosed F102 was the biggest and most powerful jet yet stationed at Gowen. The Guard flew them from 1964 until 1975.

years were Col. Martin H. Johnson, Lt. Col. David N. Johnson, Col. William P. Coburn, Kenneth E. Nordling, and Samuel E. Corn. In 1978 Brig. Gen. William A. Free was made Assistant Adjutant General, Air. Group commanders during his tenure were Col. Robert R. Corbell, II, and Ralph D. Townsend. Brig. Gen. Townsend became Assistant Adjutant General, Air, in 1989. That year Col. Gary A. Brewington was made Commander, 124th Tactical Reconnaissance Group. The present Adjutant General is Maj. Gen. Darrel V. Manning, a former State Director of Aeronautics.

All of the men listed above are pilots, and five of them saw combat duty in America's wars. They are, World War II: Lanphier, Johnson and Coburn; Viet Nam: Corbell and Townsend. Maj. Bernard F. Fisher, who began his career as an enlisted man in the Idaho Air Guard, was awarded the Congressional Medal of Honor for landing his propeller-driven air-

ISHS 65-45.13

craft under heavy fire to rescue a fellow pilot in the Viet Nam war. He retired from the Air Force in 1974 as a full colonel.[6]

The post-war era in commercial aviation was marked by tremendous growth, many new airlines, consolidation, federal deregulation, bankruptcies, and corporate takeovers. Only United Air Lines, which dates its beginnings from Varney Air Lines' April 6, 1926, airmail flight, has given Idaho continuous service since its formation in 1931 out of Varney and three other companies. Idaho's "home-grown" Empire Airlines, that began as Zimmerly, was soon absorbed, through a series of mergers, into another giant.

In 1945, at war's end, Idaho was served by United, which landed only at Boise; by Zimmerly, flying intra-state on an arc extending from Idaho Falls to Boise to Lewiston and Coeur d'Alene; by Western Airlines, formed by a merger of pioneers National Parks Airways and Western Express in 1937, serving eastern Idaho, and by Northwest Airlines, serving north Idaho out of Spokane. When Bert Zimmerly got Civil Aeronautics Board authority to go interstate with Empire Airlines in 1946, nearly all of Idaho had regularly scheduled passenger service for

ISHS 65-45.14

Idaho Falls' rustic log cabin passenger terminal and hangar are unique in Idaho. A shiny new Empire DC3 was photographed there in about 1949.

Courtesy Gwin Hicks

Empire Airline's DC3s in front of Boise's enlarged air terminal, mid 1950s. Note the unmistakable silhouette of Varney's 1931 hangar forming the bulk of the terminal.

Courtesy Boise City Archives

Passengers boarding United planes at Boise in the late '50s had a long walk across the apron, whether it was sunny, rainy, or snowy.

United Air Lines flew Convairs into smaller cities like Boise in the late 1950s.

the first time. The line's Boeing 247s were replaced with Douglas DC3s in 1948, a fleet named the *Timesavers.* After three years of successful operation, with an outstanding record of safety and performance, the CAB granted a one-year extension of certification to 1950. A three-ring circus developed when Empire, West Coast, and United Airlines all petitioned the CAB for extended routes into each other's territories. The result was a merger of West Coast and Empire, with the West Coast name continuing in use for the enlarged line. West Coast had been serving towns between Bellingham and Medford before the merger.

In 1968 West Coast became Air West through a merger with Bonanza and Pacific; after a brief period as Hughes Air West, the company was acquired in 1980 by Republic. On April 24, 1983, Republic flew its last plane out of Boise and was later absorbed into Northwest Airlines.[7]

Jet service to Idaho began October 26, 1964, with United Air Lines' Boeing 727s. The arrival of a new age in air travel prompted Boise to seek expansion of its facilities. A new

Courtesy United Air Lines

$300,000 Administration building had been completed in July, 1952, and an air traffic control tower went into use that fall. In 1967 Boise voters passed a $1.5 million bond issue by a margin of 3 to 1. Construction began in 1968 and the new terminal was dedicated in January, 1969.[8]

1969 saw intra-state service begin by Trans-Magic and Sun Valley Air. Trans-Magic was out of business by 1975. Sun Valley Air lasted only a year or two and virtually died with its owner in a fatal crash between Boise and Sun Valley that led to extensive litigation.[9]

The Airline Deregulation Act of 1978 had an immediate and drastic impact on the aviation industry in the United States. It was especially felt in Idaho, with a population of less than a million people. Without strict Civil Aeronautics Board regulation, airlines were free to pull out of small town service that was unprofitable, almost at will. Only if these towns could prove that the service provided was "essential" to their economic well-being were the airlines forced to stay. With new companies eager to fill the gaps in feeder line service, it was hard to persuade the CAB that service by a major carrier like Air West was really essential.[10]

Conversely, major carriers were now free to seek new and more profitable markets, even if it meant competing aggressively with existing large lines that had formerly had a virtual monopoly in those areas. The resulting free competition, which proponents of deregulation had said would create lower prices for consumers, and less duplication of service, actually created a chaos that resembled nothing so much as "musical chairs" with airlines. Companies that service Idaho cities were constantly coming and going. When one pulled out a new one came in. New companies, chiefly small intra-state or interstate commuter lines, competed fiercely with one another, and soon disappeared from the scene. Some merged with larger airlines or were bought out by them.

Courtesy Boise City Archives

Most went bankrupt.[11]

A sad roster of small airlines in Idaho during the period of deregulation musical chairs, and what happened to each, is a tangled web of high hopes, inexperience, undercapitalization, and occasional ineptitude. The fact that deregulation came at a time of economic recession and rising fuel costs only magnified the problems new air carriers faced.

Cascade, a Spokane company, began flying between Boise and North Idaho in the mid '70s. In 1979 they were described as "a profitable well-established commuter airline" that maintained a reasonably stable flight schedule. Cascade's only competition for the Lewiston market was Air West at that time. In 1980 the company began expansion into southeast Idaho after Western Airlines pulled out of Pocatello. By August 15, 1985, Cascade was in trouble and announced it too would abandon Pocatello. Horizon Airline said it would buy Cascade stock to keep the company going until it could take it

Courtesy Boise City Archives

Top left: The four-motored DC6B was a big advance over the DC3, but jets were just around the corner.

Top right: Beyond the Hughes Airwest DC9 can be seen Boise's new traffic control tower. It began operation in June, 1975. Above: Air Traffic Controller's view of Boise Air Terminal from the earlier tower, completed 1952.

Courtesy Boise City Archives

Above: *Air West's DC9s of the late '70s were painted bright yellow. They were popularly known as "yellow bananas."*

ISHS 72-190.46

Right: *An Air Force rescue helicopter was on display for the public open house and dedication of Boise's new terminal building, July 13, 1952.*

Courtesy United Air Lines

United Air Lines began flying DC8 jets in September, 1957. This photo was taken in 1958.

over. On March 8, 1986, Cascade quit flying and filed for Chapter 7 bankruptcy. In September the airline's equipment was sold at auction.[12]

Frontier, a successful company into the early '80s, began reducing flights in June, 1984, when 20 cities were dropped. By November, the airline was so short of cash it began cutting wages. When United pilots went on strike in May, 1985, Frontier added flights, hoping to take advantage of the temporary situation. In February, 1986, in a desperate attempt to attract business, the ailing line drastically reduced its fares — a move quickly followed by the competition. Asked how airlines that were already losing money could reduce fares to meet such a tactic, an airline agent said, "In this business we follow the lemming principle."[13] In August, 1986, Frontier shut down and filed for Chapter 11 bankruptcy.[14]

Another deregulation baby that died in infancy was Coeur d'Alene based Gem State. Even before the Act went into effect November 1, 1978, the new company had ordered three Swearingen 19-passenger Metroliner prop jets.

ISHS 77-163.65

West Coast Airlines' inaugural flight to Salt Lake with a Fairchild F27 in August, 1959, carried Nick Bez, President of West Coast, Bob Day, Mayor of Boise, and Robert E. Smylie, Governor of Idaho.

Key Airlines of Salt Lake City flew Convairs to Sun Valley in the 1970s.

Courtesy BLM/BIFC

Service was begun December 1. When Key Airline pulled out of Sun Valley in April, Gem State rushed to fill the vacancy, but was already having trouble getting fuel due to the shortage. On November 6, 1979, less than a year after it started to fly, Gem State announced plans to suspend operations three days later. Other small companies were duplicating nearly every route Gem State flew, so there was hardly a ripple when the fledgling line went under.[15]

Key Airline of Salt Lake City provided regular service to Sun Valley and McCall in the years just before deregulation. In February, 1979, the company decided to stop flying into Sun Valley in April and May, October and November, since in those slack periods it had been losing $100,000 per month due to light passenger loads. Undaunted by Key's experience, newcomers rushed in anyway and took their own lumps. By fall, Key abandoned its Sun Valley service entirely, saying that it would thereafter fly charters only.[16]

Mountain West began flying on January 15, 1979, between Boise-Reno, Salt Lake, San Jose, Pocatello and Idaho Falls, using three Brazilian made Bandeirante 18-passenger twin-engine turboprops. They, too, announced service to Sun Valley to replace Key, and eastern Idaho flights to replace those left when Gem State folded. By December, 1979, the airline told reporters it was "alive and well," despite having to lay off 38 employees, and admitted that it had not met its payroll on time twice in less than two months.[17] Bankruptcy followed.

Pacific Express of Chico, California, began Idaho service in February, 1982. The line lost $19.1 million in 1982, $12 million in 1983, and filed for bankruptcy in February, 1984. The announcement came as a complete surprise to ticket holders, and especially employees, who were told of the action on a tape-recorded message from company headquarters. "Increased competition, diminishing traffic, and a shortage of working capital" were reasons for

Courtesy Boise City Archives

Boise Air Terminal as it looked in 1966. Boise Aviation and Boise Cascade hangars are at top, old Varney hangar, remodeled into the terminal, center, and a DC3 on the apron, foreground.

Aviation Hall of Famer Grover Loening with his son Mike, a well-known speed flier who operated out of Salmon and Boise. Mike Loening was killed in a mountain crash in the mid-'70s.

Aircraft Service Co.'s Ford Trimotor made a dramatic contrast with an Air Force F86D when the two were photographed at Gowen Field in 1956.

Courtesy Idaho Air National Guard

shut-down, according to the tape. Employees were stunned by the news, and reports from cities served by the company said they were "literally in tears." Passengers left high and dry with useless tickets were more angry than tearful.[18]

Pacific Southwest opened Idaho service with cut-rate fares that attracted a flurry of travel to California just before Christmas, 1985. The company flew into Boise only until September 30, 1986.[19] Sky West, which had flown Idaho Falls-Boise, suspended service in March, 1984.[20] Transwestern Airlines, which began flying in Idaho in 1982, was merged with Horizon on January 1, 1984.[21]

Other commuter airlines that came and went in the 1970s and '80s were Air Idaho, which lost its certification because it abandoned a route without notifying the Idaho Public Utilities Commission; Air Oregon of Portland, which merged with Horizon; Big Sky went bankrupt; Columbia Airline discontinued service almost as soon as it began; Trans-Magic, which was boarding 300 passengers a month in 1970 was out of business in 1975.[22]

Larger airlines were equally unstable in the period. Air West, as noted earlier, became Hughes Air West, then Republic, and finally was absorbed by Northwest. Continental came to Idaho after acquiring Frontier, and pulled out shortly after a Denver-Boise flight crashed on takeoff killing 28, 14 of them from Idaho. In addition to litigation resulting from this disaster, due to improper de-icing procedures, Continental drew further flack in 1990 when its British ad agency promoted special-rate flights to the United States with copy that read "Admittedly there are a few places in the States we don't fly to, but be honest, how often do you really need to go to Boise, Idaho?" Both Idaho Governor Cecil Andrus and Boise Mayor Dirk Kempthorne called it a "cheap shot" that was insensitive to the feelings of Idahoans and damaging to its image. They demanded an apology, and got it from Frank Lorenzo, chairman of Texas Air which controlled Continental.[23]

Delta Airlines, now the third largest air carrier in the United States, began Boise service in 1987 after merging with Western which had been in the city since 1984.[24] Northwest Airlines, which had served North Idaho out of Spokane for many years, cut three Spokane-Seattle flights December 1, 1990, primarily because of stiff competition from Horizon Air.[25] This gave new opportunities for Empire Airlines as well. The new Empire, using the same name as Bert Zimmerly's 1946 company, began serving Idaho in 1984, and is still in business. "Idaho's Airline," as it calls itself, offers five round-trip flights daily between Boise and Coeur d'Alene with stops at Lewiston.[26]

Other developments of recent years worthy of mention are vastly improved facilities at all major Idaho airports, increased use of helicopters for a variety of services, specialized crop duster aircraft, and the emergence of hot air ballooning as a popular recreational activity.

Boise Air Terminal began a major remodeling and expansion in 1980 after voters approved a $7 million revenue-bond issue in 1979. New construction nearly doubled the capacity of the terminal, providing a new southern concourse and a total of eight jet noseloaders.[27] Don Duvall, airport manager from 1956 to 1984, capped his career with this expansion, made possible by persuading the Idaho Legislature to allow revenue-bond issues rather than general obligation bonds only, as formerly. He and his airport commission had secured a $1.5 million bond issue in 1967 by promising that "there would never be a nickel of property tax go to pay for it and there never was." Duvall is especially proud that a public entity kept its word to the taxpayers, although the skeptics all said it wouldn't.[28] John Anderson, current director of Boise Air Terminal, and the Airport Commission have ambitious plans for an entirely new terminal, runway, and other facilities on the south side of the present airport, to be built when needs warrant it.[29]

The commission, which serves without pay, has always worked closely with airport directors in planning for future growth. Those who have served, since the first commission was appointed in 1946 (see page 127), are: Walter R. Dufresne, 1950-60; Thomas R. Hardy, 1960-64; Stanley E. King, 1961-63; Gen. James S. Brooks, 1963-90; James B. Cruzen, 1964-89; H. Ferd Koch, 1972-87; Gene Nora Jessen, 1977-87; Berne K. Jensen, 1980-; H. Dean Summers, 1987-; Judy A. Bedal, 1987-; Col. Ralph E. Townsend, 1989-, and Phil Reberger, 1990.[30]

Helicopters have proven especially useful in Idaho due to the rugged mountain terrain. They are used by emergency medical units at several Idaho hospitals and have rescued hunters and accident victims statewide. Their routine work includes supplying remote mining camps, patrolling power transmission lines, surveying and mapping, and hauling skiers to virgin slopes where the powder snow is deep. Jack Hoke of Helicopters, Inc., in Boise, bought the company in 1964 when it had three turbocharged "choppers." By 1971 the business had grown to need the services of 16, including two six-passenger French Alouettes worth nearly $250,000 each. The use of helicopters in fire fighting, mentioned in Chapter XIV, has proven effective in special situations, and they are regularly used for transfer of fish and game to new locations.[31]

Crop dusting by air has been widespread over Idaho since the end of World War II, using biplanes, both high- and low-wing monoplanes, and new specialty craft designed and built in the Gem State. Dean Wilson of Boise, who has been called "a certifiable genius" with aircraft, designed the Eagle, a dramatically improved crop duster first marketed in 1981. Due to its long, glider-like wings it could laydown a wider swath than other planes. It also burned much less fuel. Although 89 Eagles were sold in a three-year period, the last one was produced in October, 1984. Two other Dean Wilson-designed planes are being manufactured in Idaho today and are selling well: The Avid Flyer, produced in Caldwell, and the Kit Fox by Denney Aerocraft in Nampa.[32]

Hot air balloons were flown in Idaho as long ago as 1892, but the modern era of ballooning began in the 1960s. In 1967 Mark Semich brought his balloon-building business to Coeur d'Alene and began to manufacture one- and four-man models in a small shop with one assistant. The Semco Balloon Co. was, in 1968, "The world's only certified manufacturer of hot air balloons." Certification came from the CAA, allowing Semich's balloons to be flown anywhere that ordinary aircraft were permitted. This, with licensed pilots, made the Semco balloons different from earlier models that had to be flown far from human habitation.[33] Gladys Buroker began flying balloons with Mark Semich in the early 1970s. (See photo, page 94.)

Courtesy United Air Lines

Top: Leon D. Cuddeback in 1926. Above: Buck Hilbert in 1976.

AVIATION HISTORY RELIVED

XVI

Celebrations of historic events, like the events that inspired them, have a way of making history too.

April 6, 1976, was the 50th anniversary of Leon D. Cuddeback's Varney Air Lines flight from Pasco to Boise to Elko with the first contract airmail. United Air Lines, which dates its own history from that day in 1926, since Varney was a United predecessor company, went all out to mark the anniversary appropriately.

With the backing of the board of the Air Transport Association, United Air Lines officials secured Post Office approval of a special commemorative stamp that read "Commercial Aviation, 1926-1976." On it were depicted a Ford monoplane and a Swallow biplane of the kind Cuddeback flew in 1926.[1]

To recreate the historic flight, an original Swallow biplane was located and carefully restored. It was found in a barn loft in Illinois where its original owners had stored it 40 years before, shortly after two accidents discouraged them from further attempts to fly it. E.E. "Buck" Hilbert, a United DC8 jet pilot and antique plane restorer from Union, Illinois, who found the old Swallow, took on the job of making it flyable again. He was the natural choice to make the golden anniversary hop from Pasco to Boise to Elko. Hilbert had to scour the country to locate replacement parts needed for the restoration. The 200 horsepower Wright J4 radial engine alone cost $5,000.[2]

The Swallow was shipped to Boise for final assembly, tuneup, and test flights. Hilbert had one forced landing and one emergency landing due to the antique Wright engine before deciding to replace it with a 1962 Model 220 horsepower Continental radial, loaned by Boise

Courtesy Al Cox

Courtesy Robert R. Auth

Top: Leon Cuddeback greets Buck Hilbert at Boise Air Terminal, April 6, 1976.
Above: Cuddeback listens to speakers laud his historic 1926 flight.

Courtesy Gwin Hicks

Courtesy Al Cox

Top: Leon Cuddeback enjoyed a good laugh with Empire Airline's pilot George Solomon when Empire picked up its first Pasco mail, 1946. Above: Thirty years later, Buck Hilbert's restored Swallow is unloaded at Boise to be prepared for the recreation of Cuddeback's 1926 flight.

plane collector Joe Terteling. The Continental was similar to the Wright in appearance. Then, on April 6, 1976, at exactly 6:23 a.m., 50 years to the minute from Cuddeback's takeoff, the little Swallow left the ground at Pasco headed for Boise. Leon Cuddeback, 77, watched the takeoff, then jetted to Boise with Richard J. Ferris, president of United, and Edward E. Carlson, chairman of the board, to greet Hilbert when he arrived.[3]

"I didn't have a thought of making history when I took off with that first 200 pounds of mail for Varney Air Lines," Cuddeback recalled. "I held up a wet finger to test the wind, decided the wind was thataway; Boise was thataway, and took off."[4]

A storm buffeted Hilbert's Swallow, forcing him to vary from Cuddeback's original route and to take three hours to get to Boise. The weather was so bad that six of the eight chase planes with photographers aboard had to turn back to Pasco or seek other landing places along the way, but Hilbert made it.[5]

Courtesy United Air Lines

In Boise, in a light rain, Idaho's first lady, Carol Andrus, christened a new United Boeing 727 the *Leon D. Cuddeback,* while the old pilot looked on. In response to glowing tributes from United chairman Carlson and Buck Hilbert, the tall white-haired pioneer spoke briefly to the crowd. "Back in 1926 we didn't have a lot of things you have today. We didn't have expense accounts, secretaries, or pensions. Most important we didn't have the knowledge available today. But with what we had, we started something big."[6] That was an understatement.

Courtesy Al Cox

Top: Buck Hilbert in the Swallow, April 6, 1976. Above: The Swallow over Boise.

Courtesy Idaho Department of Aeronautics

Glider flying over Idaho mountains is a popular sport. This Hailey-based craft is over the Sawtooths.

NOTES

I UP, UP, AND AWAY

1. *Idaho Tri-weekly Statesman,* 25 March 1882, p. 3, c. 1.
2. Ibid., 22 April 1882, p. 3, c. 1.
3. *Idaho Daily Statesman,* 12 December 1909, p. 5, c. 1-4.
4. Ibid., 2 August 1909, p. 5, c. 3.
5. Ibid., 30 August 1892, p. 8, c. 1.
6. Ibid., 24 August 1892, p. 8, c. 2.
7. Stehling, Kurt R. and Beller, William, *Skyhooks: The Story of Ballooning From 1783 to the Present,* Doubleday & Co., Garden City, N.Y., 1962, pp. 9-19.
8. *Family Encyclopedia of American History,* The Readers Digest Association, Pleasantville, N.Y., 1975, p. 646.
9. Stehling and Beller, pp. 70-74, 79-81, 84, 88-109.
10. *Idaho Daily Statesman,* 23 August 1908, p. 2, c. 1-4.
11. *1938 Britannica Book of the Year,* Encyclopaedia Britannica, Chicago, London, Toronto, 1938, pp. 201-211.
12. *Encyclopaedia Britannica,* Chicago, London, Toronto, 1938, p. 472.
13. *Idaho Daily Statesman,* 18 October 1908, Section 4, p. 1, c. 3-4.
14. Ibid., 20 October 1908, p. 3, c. 1.
15. *Weiser American,* 29 June 1911, p. 1, c. 6.
16. *Idaho Daily Statesman,* 2 September 1918, p. 2, c. 2.
17. Brochure in the collection of Robert Auth, Boise.
18. *Idaho Daily Statesman,* 7 August 1922, p. 2, c. 4.
19. Stehling and Beller, p. 188.
20. *Idaho Daily Statesman,* 15 June 1922, p. 4, c. 5-6.
21. Stehling and Beller, pp. 229-237.
22. Ibid., pp. 237-238.
23. *Idaho Daily Statesman,* 15 June 1922, p. 4, c. 5-6.
24. Ibid., 2 September 1923, p. 1, c. 2-6; p. 2, c. 1.
25. Ibid., 17 January 1925, p. 1, c. 2; 20 January 1925, p. 1, c. 6.
26. Ibid., 7 September 1925, p. 1, c. 2; 10 September 1925, p. 5, c. 1.
27. Thomas and Thomas, pp. 50-60.

II DARING YOUNG MEN, AND A GIRL

1. Arch Whitehouse, *The Early Birds,* Doubleday & Co., Garden City, N.Y., 1965, pp. 61-75.
2. *American Heritage History of Flight,* American Heritage Publishing Co., N.Y., 1962, p. 124.
3. Ibid., p. 124.
4. *Idaho Daily Statesman,* 25 September 1910, p. 9, c. 1.
5. For the best short account of Bleriot's flight, see Lowell Thomas and Lowell Thomas, Jr., *Famous First Flights That Changed History,* Doubleday & Co., Garden City, N.Y., 1968, pp. 3-17.
6. *Idaho Daily Statesman,* 27 September 1910, p. 6, c. 1.
7. Ibid., 13 October 1910, p. 3, c. 2-4.
8. Ibid., 15 October 1910, p. 3, c. 2.
9. *Lewiston Morning Tribune,* 7 October 1910, p. 5, c. 4.
10. Ibid., 14 October 1910, p. 5, c. 3-4.
11. Ibid., 6 October 1910, p. 5, c. 3.

12. Ibid., 6 October 1910, p. 5, c. 8.

13. Ibid., 2 October 1910, pp. 2, 5, 6.

14. Ibid., 2 October 1910, Section 2, p. 1.

15. John Townsend Trowbridge, *"Darius Green and His Flying Machine,"* in *The Vagabonds, and Other Poems,* Boston, Fields, Osgood & Co., 1869.

16. *Lewiston Morning Tribune,* 10 October 1910, p. 3, c. 5.

17. Ibid., 15 October 1910, p. 12, c. 3-4.

18. *Idaho Daily Statesman,* 16 October 1910, p. 1, c. 4.

19. *Lewiston Morning Tribune,* 31 July 1904, p. 7, c. 2-3.

20. Ibid., 6 October 1931: 1 June 1952, p. 12.

21. Ibid., 1 June 1952, p. 12.

22. *Idaho Daily Statesman,* 20 April 1911, p. 1, c. 7.

23. Ibid., 21 April 1911, p. 1, c. 1.

24. *American Heritage History of Flight,* p. 151.

25. *Idaho Daily Statesman,* 16 April 1911, p. 2, c. 1.

26. Whitehouse, pp. 154-155.

27. *Lewiston Morning Tribune,* 12 October 1910, p. 1, c. 5.

28. *American Heritage History of Flight,* p. 124. Martin Caidin, *Barnstorming,* Duell, Sloan & Pearce, New York, 1965, pp. 16-31. Robert G. Bailey, *River of No Return,* Bailey-Blake, Lewiston, Idaho, 1935, pp. 86-87.

29. *Idaho Daily Statesman,* 11 April 1911, p. 2, c. 6.

30. Ibid.

31. Ibid., 31 May 1913, p. 6, c. 1.

32. Ibid., 30 May 1913, p. 6, c. 3.

33. *Weekly Press-Times,* Wallace, 8 August 1913, p. 1, c. 6.

34. *Idaho Daily Statesman,* 30 May 1913, p. 6, c. 3.

35. *Weekly Press-Times,* 8 August 1913, p. 1, c. 6.

36. *Idaho Daily Statesman,* 30 May 1913, p. 6, c. 3.

37. Ibid., 23 June 1915, p. 7.

38. Ibid.

39. Ibid., 22 June 1915, p. 1, c. 5.

40. Ibid., 23 June 1915, p. 6, c. 1-3.

41. Ibid., 22 June 1915, p. 1, c. 3.

42. Ibid., 25 June 1915, p. 1, c. 1.

43. Ibid., 25 June 1915, p. 3, c. 2.

44. *Caldwell Tribune,* 27 September 1912, p. 1, c. 3-4; 4 October 1912, p. 1, c. 3-4; 11 October 1912, p. 1, c. 3. *Idaho Statesman,* 28 January 1966.

45. *Twin Falls Times,* 16 September 1913, p. 1, c. 3-4.

46. Ibid., 23 September 1913, p. 1, c. 1.

47. *Weekly Press-Times,* Wallace, 22 August 1913, p. 2, c. 1.

48. Ibid., p. 2, c. 1.

49. *Idaho Republican,* Blackfoot, 25 September 1914, p. 1, c. 1-2. The same company cancelled its appearance at Rexburg, but a substitute was found. J. Floyd Smith flew at the Rexburg Fair September 24, 30, and October 1, 1914. See David L. Crowder, *Rexburg, Idaho: The First 100 Years, 1883-1983,* Rexburg, Idaho, 1983, pp. 172-173.

50. *Idaho Daily Statesman,* 5 July 1916, p. 5, c. 1.

51. Ibid., 8 July 1916, p. 1, c. 3.

52. Ibid., 5 July 1916, p. 1, c. 5; p. 2, c. 1.

III FLYING CIRCUS

1. *Family Encyclopedia of American History,* Reader's Digest Association, Pleasantville, N.Y., 1975, p. 644.

2. *National Archives,* Record Group 18, Entry 206, File C71.6 37, unpaged.

3. Ibid.

4. *Idaho Daily Statesman,* 19 April 1919, p. 2, c. 2.

5. Ibid., 20 April 1919, p. 2, c. 1.

6. Ibid., 20 April 1919, p. 2, c. 3.

7. Ibid., 20 April 1919, p. 2, c. 2.

8. Ibid., 20 April 1919, p. 2, c. 1.

9. Ibid., 20 April 1919, p. 2, c. 1.

10. David G. Dorsey memoir, sent to author 22 February, 1991.

11. *National Archives,* loc. cit.

12. *1946 Britannica Book of the Year,* Encyclopaedia

Britannica, Chicago, London, Toronto, p. 691. *Family Encyclopedia of American History,* pp. 21-22.

IV BARNSTORMERS AND DARE-DEVILS

1. *Webster's Ninth New Collegiate Dictionary,* Merriam-Webster, Springfield, Massachusetts, 1984, p. 131.
2. Martin Caidin, *Barnstorming,* Duell, Sloan & Pearce, New York, 1965, is a romantic account of the subject, but makes no mention of the Pacific Northwest and truly great barnstormers like Tex Rankin and Nick Mamer.
3. *Idaho Daily Statesman,* p. 9, c. 5; 15 April 1920, p. 4, c. 5.
4. Ibid., 10 April 1920, p. 9, c. 5; 15 April 1920, p. 4, c. 5.
5. Ibid., 12 April 1920, p. 2, c. 7.
6. Ibid., 12 May 1920, p. 5, c. 1.
7. Ibid., 2 October 1920, p. 1, c. 1.
8. Ibid., 3 October 1920, p. 1, c. 1.
9. Ibid., 4 October 1920, p. 2, c. 5.
10. Ibid., 4 July 1921, p. 1, c. 2-3.
11. Ibid., 3 October 1921, p. 2, c. 3.
12. Ibid., 5 October 1921, p. 2, c. 6.
13. Ibid., 24 October 1921, p. 3, c. 3.
14. Ibid., 24 May 1924, p. 1, c. 1.
15. Ibid., 23 June 1925, p. 1, c. 4; 27 June 1925, p. 7, c. 5.
16. Ibid., 17 October 1925, p. 2, c. 2.
17. Ibid., 13 April 1926, p. 7, c. 1.
18. Ibid., 8 April 1926, p. 5, c. 3.
19. Ibid., 11 April 1926, p. 2, c. 3.
20. Ibid., 3 May 1926, p. 3, c. 5; May 1926, p. 4, c. 3-4.
21. Ibid., 10 September 1927, p. 7, c. 4-5.
22. Ibid., 12 September 1927, p. 1, c. 6.
23. Ibid., 13 September 1927, p. 10, c. 1.
24. Ibid., 4 October 1927, p. 7, c. 3.
25. Ibid., 28 August 1927, Sec. 2, p. 2, c. 2.
26. Ibid., 9 August 1927, p. 5, c. 5.
27. Ibid., 12 November 1928, p. 1, c. 7.
28. Ibid., 18 December 1978,
29. Ibid., 19 April 1911, p. 6, c. 1.
30. Ibid., 7 May 1928, p. 2, c. 3.
31. Ibid., 1 October 1928, p. 2, c. 1.
32. Ibid., 12 October 1928, p. 6, c. 4.
33. Ibid., 5 September 1930, p. 3, c. 4; 7 September 1930, p. 8, c. 1-2, p. 8, c. 3.
34. Ibid., 1 March 1931, p. 14, c. 5; 2 March 1931, p. 2, c. 4; 8 March 1931, p. 4, c. 3.
35. Ibid., 12 April 1931, p. 6, c. 2.
36. Ibid., 13 April 1931, p. 1, c. 7-8.
37. Ibid., 2 May 1931, p. 1, c. 8.
38. Ibid., 27 June 1931, p. 7, c. 6; 29 June 1931, p. 1, c. 1; 30 June 1931, p. 1, c. 3.
39. State of Idaho, Department of Public Works, Aeronautics Division, *Aeronautics Bulletin No. 4,* Revised to June 1, 1931, pp. 59-69. There are 50 "airports and landing fields" listed.
40. *Idaho Daily Statesman,* 10 August 1931, p. 8, c. 5-8.
41. Carl M. Cleveland, *Upside-Down Pangborn, King of the Barnstormers,* Aviation Book Company, Glendale, California, 1978, pp. 10-24.
42. David Nevin, *The Pathfinders,* Time-Life Books, Alexandria, Virginia, 1980, pp. 144-145.

V FLYING THE MAIL

1. *Family Encyclopedia of American History,* The Reader's Digest Association, Pleasantville, N.Y., 1975, p. 23.
2. Frank J. Taylor, *High Horizons,* McGraw-Hill Book Co., New York, London, Toronto, 1951, pp. 8-9.
3. *Idaho Daily Statesman,* 10 April 1920, p. 9, c. 5; 15 April 1920, p. 4, c. 5.
4. Taylor, pp. 22-23.
5. *Idaho Daily Statesman,* 12 May 1920, p. 5, c. 1.

6. Ibid., 9 October 1921, Sec. 2, p. 1.
7. Cyril C. Thompson, holograph memoir donated by Chet Moulton, now in the Idaho Historical Society Archives, pp. 3-4.
8. Ibid., p. 6.
9. Ibid., p. 7.
10. *Idaho Daily Statesman,* 26 February 1926, p. 5, c. 1; 16 March 1926, p. 10, c. 2.
11. Ibid., 1 March 1926, p. 2, c. 5.
12. Ibid.
13. Ibid., 28 March 1926, p. 4, c. 1.
14. Ibid., 18 March 1926, p. 5, c. 5; 21 March 1926, p. 4, c. 1.
15. Ibid., 30 March 1926, p. 4, c. 5.
16. Ibid., 31 March 1926, p. 6, c. 1-3.
17. Ibid., 7 April 1926, p. 1, c. 1; p. 1, c. 4; p. 2, c. 2-4; p. 2, c. 5-7.
18. Ibid., 4 April 1926, p. 4, c. 4.
19. Ibid., 6 April 1926, p. 2, c. 1.
20. Ibid., 7 April 1926, p. 1, c. 1; p. 2, c. 1.
21. Ibid., 7 April 1926, p. 2, c. 1.
22. Ibid., 8 April 1926, p. 1, c. 6-7.
23. Ibid., 9 April 1926, p. 1, c. 6.
24. Ibid.
25. United Air Lines presidents and other top brass, along with pilot Leon Cuddeback, were in Boise in 1951 and again in 1976 to celebrate the 25th and 50th anniversaries of the 1926 flight.
26. Taylor, p. 23.
27. Walter J. Boyne, *The Smithsonian Book of Flight,* Smithsonian Books, Washington, D.C., Orion Books, New York, 1987, p. 121.
28. *Idaho Daily Statesman,* 16 April 1927, p. 1, c. 7.
29. Ibid., 21 May 1927, p. 7, c. 7.
30. Ibid., 7 April 1926, p. 2, c. 5.
31. Ibid., 8 June 1927, p. 2, c. 4.
32. Ibid., 24 July 1927, Sec. 2, p. 7, c. 1-4.
33. Ibid., 22 May 1927, p. 1, c. 6.
34. Ibid., 13 June 1927, p. 5, c. 1; 22 June 1927, p. 6, c. 6; 27 June 1927, p. 8, c. 4.
35. *Caldwell News-Tribune,* 20 January 1965, p. 8, c. 1-3.
36. *Idaho Daily Statesman,* 16 January 1928, p. 1, c. 7; 20 January 1928, p. 1, c. 6.
37. Ibid., 22 January 1928, p. 1, c. 7; 23 January 1928, p. 1, c. 5.
38. Ibid., 23 January 1928, p. 1, c. 3.
39. Ibid.
40. Ibid., 2 March 1928, p. 9, c. 4; 30 May 1928, p. 2, c. 2-4.
41. Ibid., 12 March 1928, p. 2, c. 3.
42. Ibid.
43. Ibid., 8 March 1928, Sec. 2, p. 1.
44. Ibid.
45. Ibid., 3 July 1928, p. 10, c. 1.
46. Ibid., 22 July 1928, p. 1, c. 3-5.
47. Ibid., 24 November 1928, p. 1, c. 1.
48. Ibid., 27 July 1928, p. 5, c. 3; 29 July 1928, p. 14, c. 1.
49. Ibid., 5 September 1928, p. 1, c. 7; 6 September 1928, p. 1, c. 7.
50. Ibid., 22 December 1928, p. 5, c. 2.
51. Ibid., 18 January 1929, p. 1, c. 7; 19 January 1929, p. 1, c. 8; 20 January 1929, p. 1, c. 7; 21 January 1929, p. 1, c. 7.
52. *Antique Airplane Association News,* March, 1964, pp. 8-9.
53. *Idaho Daily Statesman,* 8 February 1929, p. 9, c. 5.
54. Ibid., 4 February 1928, p. 1, c. 5.
55. Ibid., 23 August 1930, p. 1, c. 4.
56. Evans Kerrigan, *American Medals and Decorations,* Mallard Press, New York, 1990, p. 73.
57. *Idaho Daily Statesman,* 29 December 1932, p. 1, c. 7.
58. Information furnished by Robert Auth from notes written by pioneer Boise flier and airport manager Ivan Nelson.
59. *Idaho Daily Statesman,* 5 June 1932, p. 2, c. 5-6.

VI MOUNTAIN PILOTS

1. *Idaho Daily Statesman,* 2 May 1920, p. 5, c. 1.
2. Ibid., 21 February 1925, p. 1, c. 4.
3. Ibid., 5 April 1925, p. 1, c. 2; 4 April 1926, sec. 2, p. 10.
4. Ibid., 19 August 1925, p. 2, c. 3; 21 August 1925, p. 2, c. 3.
5. Ibid., 14 September 1925, p. 2, c. 4.
6. Ibid., 16 September 1925, p. 2, c. 1.
7. Ibid., 11 April 1926, sec. 2, p. 1.
8. Ibid., 13 June 1927, p. 5, c. 1.
9. Ibid., 25 December 1928, p. 8, c. 1.
10. Ibid., 31 January 1929, p. 3, c. 2.
11. Ibid., 8 October 1928, p. 7, c. 6.
12. Ibid., 27 October 1928, p. 1, c. 1; 29 October 1928, p. 1, c. 2, 1 November 1928, p. 1, c. 1-2.
13. Ibid., 25 October 1928, p. 2, c. 1.
14. Ibid., 13 January 1931, p. 7, c. 4; 17 January 1931, p. 7, c. 4.
15. Ibid., 18 January 1931, p. 7, c. 1-2.
16. Ibid., 19 February 1931, p. 3, c. 5; 1 March 1931, p. 6, c. 4.
17. Ibid., 16 March 1931, p. 1, c. 1.
18. Ibid., 1 November 1931, p. 1, c. 1; 10 November 1931, p. 1, c. 6.
19. Ibid., 13 November 1931, p. 5, c. 2; 2 December 1931, p. 1, c. 4.
20. Ibid., 24 December 1931, p. 8, c. 1.
21. Ibid., 19 January 1932, p. 3, c. 1; 6 February 1932, p. 7, c. 3; 21 February 1932, p. 3, c. 5; 16 March 1932, p. 1, c. 1-2.
22. Steve Smith, *Fly the Biggest Piece Back,* Mountain Press, Missoula, Montana, 1975, p. 107.
23. Ibid., p. 108.
24. Ibid., p. 115.
25. Ibid., p. 105.
26. *Idaho Daily Statesman,* 8 May 1932, sec. 2, p. 1.
27. *Newsweek,* 6 August 1979, pp. 50-51; *Time,* 14 January 1985, p. 8.
28. Quoted in Smith, p. 129.
29. *Idaho Daily Statesman,* 14 February 1943.
30. *Chicago Tribune,* 15 February 1943.
31. *Idaho Daily Statesman,* 14 February 1943.
32. Letters in Penn Stohr's scrapbooks, loaned by his sons, Dan and Penn Stohr, Jr., and quoted by permission.
33. *Idaho Daily Statesman,* undated clipping, fall, 1943. Conversation with John Corlett, 28 July 1991.
34. Ibid.
35. Marian Templeton Place and Larry Florek, *Tall Timber Pilots,* Viking Press, New York, 1953, p. 84.
36. Telephone conversation with Jim Larkin, 9 July 1991. Conversation with Randy Woods, 8 July 1991.
37. Conversation with Harold Dougal, 1 July 1991.
38. *Rudder Flutter,* May, 1967, pp. 4-5. Conversations with Glenn Higby and Jim Larkin, 9 July 1991, 12 July 1991.
39. Conversations with Chet Moulton 9-10 July 1991.

VII PIONEER PASSENGER CARRIERS

1. *Boise Capital News,* 18 April 1929.
2. *Ninth Biennial Report, Department of Public Works, State of Idaho,* 31 December 1936, p. 155.
3. *Idaho Daily Statesman,* 31 January 1929, p. 6, c. 2.
4. Ibid., 13 April 1929.
5. Ibid., 8 April 1928, p. 13, c. 1-3.
6. Ibid., 13 April 1929.
7. Ibid., 7 June 1929, p. 1, c. 7.
8. *Boise Capital News,* 16 June 1929.
9. Ibid., 17 June 1929.
10. *Idaho Daily Statesman,* 21 June 1929.
11. *Boise Capital News,* 27 May 1929.
12. *Idaho Daily Statesman,* 5 June 1929.
13. *Boise Capital News,* 2 May 1929, 7 May 1929, 8 May 1929, 27 May 1929, 4 June 1929, 10 June 1929.

14. Ibid., 7 July 1929; *Idaho Daily Statesman,* 29 July 1929.

15. Frank Taylor, *High Horizons,* pp. 46-47; Barrett Tillman in *American Aviation Historical Society Journal,* Winter 1971. "Six Million Miles," p. 247.

16. Michael J.H. Taylor, *Boeing,* Jane's, London, 1982, p. 103.

17. Frank Taylor, p. 194.

18. Michael J. Taylor, p. 104.

19. *Idaho Daily Statesman,* 13 April 1933, p. 3, c. 1-5.

20. Ibid., 28 April 1933, p. 1, c. 4.

21. Ibid., 20 May 1933, p. 5, c. 2-3.

22. Ibid., 24 July 1931, p. 7, c. 6.

23. Frank Taylor, p. 105, 110-112.

24. *Idaho Daily Statesman,* 18 June 1965; 21 January 1969.

25. Ibid., 19 March 1939, p. 9, c. 3.

26. *Christian Science Monitor,* 19 October 1939.

27. *Idaho Daily Statesman,* 14 March 1936, p. 6, c. 10: 17 March 1936, p. 2, c. 2.

28. Don C. Wigton, *From Jenny to Jet,* Clymer, Los Angeles, 1963, p.. 101, 103.

VIII FAMOUS VISITORS

1. *Idaho Daily Statesman,* 20 July 1927, p. 3, c. 3; 25 August 1927, p. 2, c. 1; 27 August 1927, p. 10, c. 1.

2. Ibid., 5 September 1927, p. 10, c. 1.

3. Ibid.

4. David Nevin, *The Pathfinders,* Time-Life Books, Alexandria, Virginia, 1980, pp. 139, 170-171.

5. *Idaho Daily Statesman,* 10 September 1930, p. 10, c. 3; 12 September 1930, p. 1, c. 7; 22 September 1930, p. 3, c. 5-6.

6. Ibid., 26 September 1930, p. 1, c. 7; p. 10, c. 1-2.

7. Ibid., 6 May 1931, p. 5, c. 6; 14 May 1931; p. 1, c. 4.

8. Ibid., 9 January 1932, p. c. 3-6.

9. Ibid., 29 June 1932, p. 7, c. 4-5; 4 July 1932, p. 8.

10. Ibid., 4 May 1933, p. c. 8.

IX WOMEN IN IDAHO SKIES

1. *Idaho Daily Statesman,* 31 May 1913, p. 6, c. 1.

2. Ibid., 4 July 1921, p. 1, c. 2-3.

3. Ibid., 18 July 1927, p. 1, c. 6; 31 July 1927, Dec. 2, p. 11.

4. Ibid., 9 March 1928, p. 2, c. 2-3.

5. Ibid., 20 April 1928, p. 2, c. 4.

6. Ibid.

7. Ibid., 15 March 1928, p. 5, c. 3.

8. Ibid., 10 May 1928, p. 9, c. 3.

9. Ibid., 21 July 1928, p. 3, c. 4.

10. Ibid., 6 August 1928, p. 7, c. 1.

11. Valerie Moolman, *Women Aloft,* Time-Life Books, Alexandria, Virginia, 1981, pp. 45-46.

12. *Boise Capital News,* May 1930.

13. *Idaho Daily Statesman,* 26 September 1930, p. 5, c. 1.

14. *Boise Capital News,* 13 July 1930.

15. *Idaho Daily Statesman,* 9 April 1931, p. 5, c. 3; 15 April 1931, p. 7, c. 1.

16. Ibid., 27 June 1931, p. 7, c. 6; 29 June 1931, p. 1, c. 1; 30 June 1931, p. 1, c. 3.

17. Ibid., 23 October 1931, p. 1.

18. *This Fabulous Century, the Thirties,* Time-Life Books, New York, 1969, pp. 100, 110-111.

19. Frank J. Taylor, *High Horizons,* McGraw Hill, New York, London, Toronto, 1951, pp. 69-71.

20. *Idaho Daily Statesman,* 9 April 1944, p. 8.

21. Frank Taylor, p. 71.

22. Ibid.

23. *Idaho Daily Statesman,* 18-20 January 1939.

24. Ibid., 22 January 1939, p. 1, c. 1-2.

25. Ibid., 2 May 1939.

26. R. Starr Farish, letter to the author, 21 December 1989.

27. *Idaho Daily Statesman,* 23 March 1939, p. 2, c. 4.

28. Ibid., 5 May 1940.
29. Ibid., 13 May 1940, p. 3, c. 2.
30. Ibid., 25 May 1940, p. 1, c. 1.
31. Ibid., 28 May 1940, p. 1, c. 2-3.
32. Ibid., 5 June 1940, p. 1, c. 4-5.
33. Ibid., 7 November 1940, p. 6, c. 2-3.
34. Ibid., 29 June 1940, p. 2, c. 4.
35. Ibid., 27 April 1941, sec. 2, p. 4.
36. Ibid., 30 June 1940, p. 5, c. 3-5.
37. Ibid., 25 June 1940, p. 8, c. 3.
38. Ibid., 1 July 1940, p. 1, c. 4.
39. Ibid., 12 August 1940, p. 6, c. 2-4; 10 September 1940, p. 2, c. 2; 13 September 1940, p. 6, c. 1; 21 September 1940, p. 10, c. 1.
40. Ibid., 29 September 1940, p. 3, c. 3-4.
41. Ibid., 3 October 1940, p. 6, c. 3-5.
42. Ibid., 30 October 1940, p. 5, c. 7.
43. Walter J. Boyne, *The Smithsonian Book of Flight,* Washington, D.C., 1987, pp. 159-163.
44. Moolman, pp. 141-144.
45. Ibid., p. 151.
46. *Britannica Book of the Year, 1943,* Encyclopaedia Britannica, Chicago, 1943, p. 91.
47. Gene Nora Jessen, *History of the Ninety-Nines, Inc.,* The Ninety-Nines, 1979, pp. 9-11.
48. *Rudder Flutter,* May 1954, pp. 1, 5; *The Idaho 99's,* new bulletins, March, May, June, 1955; *Idaho Daily Statesman,* 17 October 1954, p. 16, c. 4-5. Kathy Albano, *Jennies to Jets: History of Aviation in the Pocatello Area,* Idaho State University Press, Pocatello, undated, but circa 1971, p. 3-5.
49. Betty Penson in *Idaho Daily Statesman,* 22 October 1978, sec. G, p. 10, c. 1-4; 29 October 1978, sec. G, p. 10, c. 1-4.
50. Gene Nora Jessen in *Idaho Daily Statesman,* 10 August 1969.
51. Conversation with Barbara Morgan, 17 July 1991.

X IDAHO STATE AERONAUTICS

1. *Idaho Session Laws* 1929, Chapter 137.
2. *Department of Public Works, Sixth Biennial Report,* 31 December 1931, p. 189.
3. *Idaho Daily Statesman,* 4 June 1931, p. 3, c. 3.
4. Ibid., 29 June 1932, p. 1, c. 2-3.
5. Ibid.
6. Ibid., 11 July 1932, p. 2, c. 2.
7. Ibid., 27 September 1932, p. 7, c. 1.
8. Ibid., 28 September 1932, p. 7, c. 3.
9. Ibid., 1 November 1932, p. 7, c. 8.
10. *Department of Public Works, Ninth Biennial Report,* 31 December 1936, p. 160.
11. Ibid., *Tenth Biennial Report,* 31 December 1938, pp. 103-105.
12. Ibid., *Eleventh Biennial Report,* 31 December 1940, p. 89.
13. Conversations with Chet Moulton 28-29 July 1991.
14. *Rudder Flutter,* September 1970, p. 8.
15. Ibid., February 1974, pp. 2-3.
16. *Department of Public Works, Fifteenth Biennial Report,* 31 December 1948, p. 5.
17. *Idaho Daily Statesman,* 20 March 1970, p. 19, c. 8; 1 July 1970, p. 1 D, c. 1.
18. Ibid., 11 April 1971, p. 1 D, c. 5-8.
19. Ibid., 4 May 1971, p. 1, c. 1-5.
20. Information supplied by State Aeronautics and by Worthie Rauscher, 29-30 July 1991.

XI COYOTE HUNTERS

1. *Idaho Daily Statesman,* 2 March 1938, p. 2, c. 4-5.
2. Ibid., 3 February 1940, p. 1, c. 1; 7 February 1940, p. 10, c. 6.
3. Ibid., 19 April 1940, p. 1, c. 5.
4. Ibid., 13 January 1941, p. 2, c. 3.
5. Ibid., 7 February 1941, p. 9, c. 4.

XII PREPARING FOR WAR

1. *Family Encyclopedia of American History,* The Reader's Digest Association, Pleasantville, N.Y., 1975, p. 639.
2. *Idaho Daily Statesman,* 25 May 1940, p. 1, c. 1.
3. Ibid., 5 September 1940.
4. Ibid., 10 February 1940, p. 2, c. 1; 12 August 1940; Ray Crowder scrapbooks.
5. Ibid., 30 October 1940, p. 3, c. 1; 3 November 1940, p. 3, c. 6-8.
6. Ibid., 29 March 1940, p. 10, c. 6; Conversation with General James Trail, 21 July 1991.
7. Conversation with Doris Willey Crowder, 21 July 1991.
8. *Idaho Daily Statesman,* 5 May 1940, p. 6, c. 2-4.
9. Conversation with Chet Moulton, June 1991, in which he called Platt "one of the best pilots I ever knew."
10. *Idaho Daily Statesman,* 28 May 1940, p. 1, c. 2-3.
11. Ibid., 25 June 1940, p. 9, c. 5.
12. Ibid., 17 July 1940, p. 7, c. 1-2.
13. Ibid., 4 October 1940, p. 1, c. 7-8.
14. Ibid., 9 October 1940, p. 6, c. 5.
15. Ibid., 4 October 1940, p. 2, c. 1.
16. Ibid., 13 October 1940, p. 5, c. 4; 17 October 1940, p. 12, c. 2.
17. Ibid., 13 November 1940, p. 1, c. 1-2.
18. Ibid., 10 January 1941, p. 1, c. 7-8; 18 January 1941, p. 1, c. 3.
19. Ibid., 16 January 1941, p. 1, c. 3.
20. Ibid., 19 January 1941, p. 9, c. 6-8.
21. *1942 Britannica Book of the Year,* Encyclopaedia Britannica, Inc., Chicago, 1942, p. 673.
22. *Idaho Daily Statesman,* 29 January 1941, p. 2, c. 1.
23. Ibid., 5 February 1941, p. 12, c. 1.
24. David Nevin, *The Pathfinders,* Time-Life Books, Alexandria, Virginia, 1980, pp. 40-49.
25. *Idaho Daily Statesman,* 11 March 1941, p. 1, c. 2-3.
26. Ibid., 15 March 1941, p. 1.
27. Ibid., 20 March 1941, p. 1, c. 4-5.
28. Ibid., 24 March 1941, p. 3, c. 3.
29. Interview with Westerman Whillock, 19 December 1990.
30. *Idaho Daily Statesman,* 18 March 1941, p. 6, c. 4-5.
31. Ibid., 27 April 1941, p. 6, c. 2-3.
32. Ibid., 23 July 1941; *Idaho Press Tribune,* 14 July 1985.
33. M/Sgt. Mac Everett *History of Gowen Field,* unpublished manuscript, Idaho Air National Guard, September 1990, p. 32.
34. Michael J.H. Taylor, *Boeing,* Jane's, London, 1982, p. 112.

XIII THE WAR YEARS

1. *Idaho Daily Statesman,* 8 December 1941, p. 1, c. 4-5.
2. Ibid., c. 4.
3. Ibid., p. 2, c. 1.
4. Ibid., p. 2, c. 2.
5. Ibid., p. 6, c. 1-2.
6. Ibid., 10 December 1941, p. 5, c. 1.
7. Ibid., 1 January 1943, p. 13, c. 2.
8. Ibid., p.13, c. 3.
9. Garry L. Fry in *American Aviation Historical Society Journal,* Fourth Quarter, 1978, "Boise Bee: The Duane Beeson Story," pp. 243-259.
10. *Idaho Daily Statesman,* 19 January 1928, p. 3, c. 2.
11. Ibid., 1 January 1943, pp. 13-16, Year-end summary of events of 1942.
12. Kathy Albano, *Jennies to Jets: History of Aviation in the Pocatello Area.* Idaho State University, undated, ca. 1971, pp. 31-32.
13. *Idaho Daily Statesman,* 1 January 1943, pp. 13-16; Year-end summary of events of 1942; 7 January 1943, p. 1, c. 4-7.
14. Michael J. H. Taylor, *Boeing,* Jane's, London, 1982, pp. 136-137.

15. *Idaho Daily Statesman,* 1 January 1943, pp. 13-16.
16. Ibid., 7 January 1943, p. 1, c. 4-7.
17. Ibid., 16 January 1943, p. 1, c. 3.
18. Ibid., 26 January 1943, p. 3, c. 5.
19. Ibid., 4 February 1943, p. 1, c. 2.
20. Ibid., 1 April 1943, p. 1, c. 1; 3 April 1943, p. 1, c. 2-3; 6 April 1943, p. 1, c. 1-2.
21. Ibid., 14 April 1943, p. 1, c. 3.
22. Ibid., 20 May 1943, p. 1, c. 6-7.
23. Ibid., 14 February 1943.
24. Conversations with Emily Foster Riley and Florence McCord, 7-8 August 1991. *Idaho Daily Statesman,* 8 August 1943, p. 10, c. 1.
25. *Idaho Daily Statesman,* 2 January 1944, pp. 6-9, Year-end summary of events of 1943.
26. Ibid., 1 January 1945; Year-end summary of events of 1944.
27. Ibid., 11 April 1944, p. 1, c. 7.
28. Information supplied by Gwin Hicks, 15 January 1991.
29. *Wallace Press-Times,* 26 May 1944.
30. *Lewiston Morning Tribune,* 11 April 1944, p. 10, c. 1.
31. Information in Bert Zimmerly scrapbooks, supplied to author by Bert Zimmerly, Jr., January, 1991. Clipping from newspapers in several northwest cities.

XIV FLYING FIRE FIGHTERS

1. Earl Cooley, *Trimotor and Trail,* Mountain Press, Missoula, 1984, pp. 22-23.
2. Ibid., p. 20.
3. Ibid., p. 26.
4. *Idaho Daily Statesman,* 19 May 1980, p. 5, c. 2-3; Cooley, p. 19.
5. Ibid., 4 August 1940, sec. 2, p. 1.
6. Ibid.
7. Jack F. Wilson, "The Wings of Fire," in *Fire Management Notes,* 1988, Vol. 49, No. 1, p. 18.
8. Ibid., p. 20.
9. Information supplied by Arnold Hartigan, BIFC.
10. Jack F. Wilson, "Rotary Wings of Fire," in *Fire Management Notes,* 1987, Vol. 48, No. 4, pp. 29-31.
11. Information supplied by Arnold Hartigan, BIFC.
12. Ibid.

XV BIGGER AND FASTER

1. *Idaho Daily Statesman,* 1 January 1946, year-end summary of events of 1945, pp. 11-13.
2. Boise Airport Commission files.
3. Master Sgt. Mac Everett, *A History of the Idaho National Guard,* 1 September 1990 draft, p. 40.
4. Ibid., pp. 23-25.
5. Conversation with Mac Everett 6 August 1991.
6. Everett, pp. 41-51, p. 15.
7. Information furnished by Gwin Hicks and Bert Zimmerly, Jr., January, 1991.
8. Interview with Don Duvall, 15 March 1990, and many subsequent conversations.
9. Conversations with Joseph Imhoff and R.B. Kading, Jr., 14-15 August 1991.
10. *Idaho Daily Statesman,* 19 November 1979, p. 8A.
11. Boise Air Terminal records.
12. *Idaho Daily Statesman,* 19 November 1979, p. 8A; 21 August 1985; 8 March 1986; 28 April 1986.
13. Conversation with George Alvarez, 13 August 1991.
14. Boise Air Terminal records; *Idaho Daily Statesman,* 24 June 1984; 27 November 1984; 30 May 1985; 11 February 1986; 29 August 1986.
15. Ibid., 11 July 1978; 3 October 1978; 24 February 1979; 25 May 1979; 6 November 1979; 19 November 1979.
16. Ibid., 24 February 1979; 25 May 1979; 19 November 1979, p. 8A.
17. Ibid., 19 October 1978; 24 February 1979; 19 November 1979; 24 December 1979.
18. Ibid., 3 February 1984; 4 February 1984.
19. Ibid., 4 February 1986, p. 63; Idaho Business Review, 15 September 1986.

20. Boise Air Terminal records.
21. Ibid.,
22. *Airport World,* July 1970, p. 21; Boise Air Terminal records.
23. *Idaho Daily Statesman,* 1990.
24. Boise Air Terminal records.
25. *Idaho Daily Statesman,* 22 October 1990.
26. Current airline schedule, 1 September 1991.
27. *Idaho Daily Statesman,* 28 February 1980, p. 5B.
28. Taped interview with Don Duvall, 15 March 1990.
29. *Idaho Daily Statesman,* 23 April 1989, p. 1E.
30. Boise Air Terminal records.
31. *Idaho Daily Statesman,* Jack Hoke interview, 1972.
32. Ibid., Tim Woodward column, 28 March 1982; Eagle Aircraft brochures furnished by Chet Bowers.
33. *Coeur d'Alene Press,* 9 January 1968, p. 6.

XVI AVIATION HISTORY RELIVED

1. *Friendly Times,* April, 1976. p. 14.
2. *Idaho Daily Statesman,* 25 March 1976, p. Fl.
3. Portland *Oregonian,* 7 April 1976, p. 1A.
4. Ibid.
5. *Idaho Daily Statesman,* 7 April 1976, p. 1A.
6. *Friendly Times,* May, 1976, p. 9.

Courtesy Bob King, Jr.

Bob King, with goggles and helmet, flew the mail to Atlanta for A.A. Bennett in the 1930s. The plane is a Zenith.

Courtesy Bob King, Jr.

Bob King with a Travelair.

Courtesy Bob King, Jr.

Bennett Air Transport Travelair at Atlanta.

Courtesy Bob King, Jr.

Bob King, left, piloted Capital Air Lines' first passenger flight in a Beech staggerwing, 1936.

BIBLIOGRAPHY

Albano, Kathy, *Jennies to Jets: History of Aviation in the Pocatello Area,* Idaho State University, Pocatello, Idaho. Undated, ca. 1971.

Boyne, Walter J., *The Smithsonian Book of Flight,* Smithsonian Books, Washington, D.C., Orion Books, New York, 1987.

Caidin, Martin, *Barnstorming,* Duell, Sloan and Pearce, New York, 1965.

Cleveland, Carl M., *Upside Down Pangborn, King of the Barnstormers,* Aviation Books, Glendale, California, 1978.

Cooley, Earl, *Trimotor and Trail,* Mountain Press, Missoula, Montana, 1984.

Dwiggins, Don, *The Air Devils,* Lippincott, New York, 1966.

Emerson, Tom, *Seaplanes from Coeur d'Alene,* self-published, Coeur d'Alene, 1973.

Jessen, Gene Nora, *History of the Ninety-Nines,* Ninety-Nines, Inc., New York, 1979.

Kerrigan, Evans, *American Medals and Decorations,* Mallard Press, New York, 1990.

Mills, Stephen E., and Phillips, James W., *Sourdough Sky: A Pictorial History of Flights and Flyers in the Bush Country,* Superior, Seattle, 1969.

Moolman, Valerie, *Women Aloft,* Time-Life Books, Alexandria, Virginia, 1981.

Nevin, David, *The Pathfinders,* Time-Life Books, Alexandria, Virginia, 1980.

Place, Marian Templeton, and Florek, Larry, *Tall Timber Pilots,* Viking Press, New York, 1953.

Smith, Steve, *Fly the Biggest Piece Back,* Mountain Press, Missoula, Montana, 1979.

Sunderman, James F. (editor), *Early Air Pioneers: 1862-1935,* Franklin Watts, New York, 1961.

Taylor, Frank, *High Horizons: Daredevil Flying Postmen to Modern Magic Carpet -- the United Air Lines Story,* McGraw-Hill, New York, London, Toronto, 1951.

Taylor, Michael J.H., *Boeing,* Jane's Publishing Co., Ltd., London, 1982.

Thomas, Lowell, and Thomas, Lowell, Jr., *Famous First Flights That Changed History,* Doubleday & Co., Garden City, N.Y., 1968.

White, Wayne E., *A History of Aviation in Idaho,* Boise State University, Boise, Idaho, 1976.

Whitehouse, Arch, *The Early Birds,* Doubleday & Co., Garden City, N.Y., 1965.

Wigton, Don C., *From Jenny to Jet: Pictorial Histories of the World's Great Airlines,* Floyd Clymer, Los Angeles, California, 1963.

Wiley, Frank W., *Montana and the Sky,* Montana Aeronautics Commission, Helena, Montana, 1966.

ISHS 80-57.17/a

Bradley Field was built west of Boise in 1945 by Aircraft Service Co., Jack Bradley, president. When it closed in 1973 it was operated by Capital Flying Service.

ACKNOWLEDGMENTS

WINGS OVER IDAHO could not have been written without the enthusiastic interest and generous support of many people. First, my warm thanks to the Boise Airport Commission, whose initial suggestion got the project going, and whose financial support made publication possible. General James S. Brooks, then chairman of the Commission, was a delight to work with, as were airport director John Anderson and business manager Linnae Costello. Mayor Dirk Kempthorne and members of the Boise City Council were supportive of the project and urged us to proceed.

Key individuals whose assistance was invaluable during initial research were Don A. Duvall, longtime airport director, whose personal involvement with Boise aviation for over 30 years made him a treasure house of information; Don Haache, Boise City Archivist, who took over management of historic airport records for preservation and cataloging; Chet Moulton, veteran director of the Idaho Department of Aeronautics, who generously shared valuable photographs and documents that will be deposited in the Idaho Historical Society, and whose wise counsel was enlisted frequently, and the reference staff at Boise Public Library, where I virtually lived for most of a year: William J. Wilson, Michie Crane, Holly Huff and Jason Reuer.

Volunteers who joined me early on in digging out aviation items from newspaper microfilm, made it possible for the book to come out in 1991. Had I scanned the papers alone for as many years as had to be covered, it might have taken another three years. The dedication and friendship of Willard and Barbara Heath, G.M. "Bud" Keyt, and David Robertson is much appreciated. Bill and Dave are United Air Lines retirees who knew personally some of the pioneers of the book.

I was privileged to consult frequently by telephone with a number of veteran aviation people, many of whom loaned photographs and other materials that have greatly enriched this book and a growing archive of Idaho aviation history. My special thanks go to Nat Adams, Del Aldecoa, Mrs. Ray Arnold, Mary Atherton, Chet Bowers, Lana Boxburger, Sylvia Burkey, Gladys Buroker, Lt. Col. Loren Call, Glen Chaney, John Collias, Al Cox, Doris Willy Crowder, Bob Day, Harold Dougal, Warren Ellison, M. Sgt. Mac Everett, Phil Gardner, Tiana Glen, Arnold Hartigan, Pearl Parsons Hayes, Gwin Hicks, Helen and Glenn Higby, Gene Nora Jessen, Ralph Johnston, James H. Jones, Bob King, Jr., Bob LaMontagne, Jim Larkin, Dr. Jim Mann, Florence McCord, Barbara Morgan, Bill Miller, Worthie Rauscher, James Read, Don and Emily Riley, Jim Robertson, Dan Stohr, Penn Stohr, Jr., Margaret Pinneo Tillotson, Gen. James Trail, Betty Penson Ward, Wayne E. White, A.G. Witter, Randy Woods, and Bert Zimmerly, Jr.

As always, in any historical undertaking, I have relied on the fine collections at the Idaho State Historical Society and the staff of the library there. Thanks to Guila Ford, Elizabeth Jacox, and John Yandell. I am also indebted to the Board of Directors of Historic Boise, Inc., publishers of this book: Robert Aldridge, Robert R. Auth, Mark Falconer, Linda Hildeman, Ernest Lombard, Lorry Roberts, Susan Stacy, and Jean Wilson.

Wings Over Idaho is dedicated to Robert R. Auth, a friend of many years who has known, loved, and collected Idaho aviation lore longer than anyone I know. Thanks, Bob, for all you have done to keep Idaho aviation history alive.

Finally, and by no means least, my love and appreciation to my wife, Novella Dee, who worked on this book as long and as hard as I did, as word processor, editor and counselor.

Arthur A. Hart

Courtesy BLM/BIFC

Evergreen International's great old restored Ford Trimotor attracted crowds when it came to Boise in May, 1990, to help celebrate National Transportation Week and BIFC's 25th Anniversary. Penn Stohr, Jr., was the pilot.

INDEX

A

B

Department of Aeronautics

Among Idaho airports to make major improvements in recent years is Twin Falls' Joslin Field.

C

D

E

F

G

H

I

J

K

L

M

N

O

P

Q

R

S

T

U

V

W

Y

Z